THE SEVEN SHIRES WAY

*A 234 mile walk around the county boundary of
Oxfordshire using public rights of way*

Elaine Steane

2002

REARDON PUBLISHING
56 Upper Norwood Street,
Cheltenham, GL53 0DU
www.reardon.co.uk

Copyright, text, Elaine Steane © 2002

Copyright, illustrations, John Steane © 2002

ISBN 1-873877-51-X
Copyright © 2002

Written and researched by Elaine Steane

Illustrations by John Steane

Design and layout by Marion Stockton
Bletchington, OX5 3DA

Printed by Information Press, Oxford

Acknowledgements

It is the friendship, enjoyment of open spaces and general merriment gained from being a member of the Oxfordshire Ramblers Association that has been the inspiration for the development of this guide.

Friends from this group of walkers made up the core team who helped design and walk the first circuit. They are Mary Barber, Bruce Finlay, Mary Francome, Richard Hardy, John Steane, and Mike & Alison Willson. Their dedication to the project meant that they were at a given grid reference on cold wintry mornings.

Then came the re-walking and checking of the route, a 234 mile long task each time, my thanks to Barry Ellis, Pat Cameron and Norman Smith, the latter of whom would often combine two days into one, 24 mile walk per day.

Our enjoyment of the route was greatly enriched by the stories and village history told to us by farmers and the local people. Our thanks to them for their interest in our boundary walking and the welcome that they gave us. I have also drawn on the expertise and local knowledge of fellow ramblers – Alan Cobb and Wendy Lines are just two of many.

The proof reading has resulted in bringing in more skills: thanks to Sue Weston, Pam & John Roberts and to Roger & Kathy Benson, also to my parents for their geographical input.

Preparation of the route on the OS maps has been done by Bill Willett, cartographer, and Joe Little, illustrator. The initial typing of the text was done by Melanie Fyson and the page layout and cover design by Marion Stockton. Thanks also, to Nicholas Reardon of Reardon Publishing for his expert assistance with the marketing and distribution, and to David Brown of Oxbow Books for his invaluable advice.

I conclude by paying tribute to my husband, John, who has combined most of the roles above as well as being illustrator. Making pencil drawings in the field has meant needing to retreat to the nearest pub to thaw out.

I welcome your comments, revisions required, and any extra information you may have on the places passed through. Most of all, I hope that you enjoy the walk.

Elaine Steane
April 2002

Care for the Countryside

Please respect the Country Code in the following ways:

- Enjoy the route, but keep to the rights of way.

- Close all gates and avoid damage to crops. Please keep away from farm animals.

- To avoid disturbance to wildlife or farm animals, keep your dog under close control at all times, preferably on a lead through fields with animals in.
  (**NB** if you are being harassed by cattle, it may be safer only in this circumstance to let the dog off the lead).

- Please take all your litter home. It looks unsightly and can be dangerous to wildlife and farm animals.

- Take extra care on country roads. Walk on the right side except round blind corners.

- If travelling by car to rendezvous points, please park carefully in order not to obstruct gateways or cause a danger to other road users.

- **Be prepared!** Carry a compass (all the map sections in the guide are north orientated). Always carry a rucksack with some warm and waterproof clothing, plenty of water, a flask of hot liquid in winter, and sun protection in the form of a hat, long-sleeved shirt and sun-screen for summer.

CONTENTS

	The Making of Oxfordshire	vi
Day One	Moreton-in-Marsh to Ascott	1
Day Two	Ascott to Edgehill	11
Day Three	Edgehill to Claydon	21
Day Four	Claydon to Middleton Cheney	31
Day Five	Middleton Cheney to Souldern	39
Day Six	Souldern to Finmere	48
Day Seven	Finmere to Ludgershall	57
Day Eight	Ludgershall to Waterperry	68
Day Nine	Waterperry to Henton	79
Day Ten	Henton to Northend	87
Day Eleven	Northend to Henley-on-Thames	95
Day Twelve	Henley-on-Thames to Tilehurst	104
Day Thirteen	Tilehurst to Moulsford	114
Day Fourteen	Moulsford to West Ilsley	123
Day Fifteen	West Ilsley to Fawley	132
Day Sixteen	Fawley to Ashdown House	141
Day Seventeen	Ashdown House to Sevenhampton	151
Day Eighteen	Sevenhampton to Southrop	161
Day Nineteen	Southrop to Great Barrington	170
Day Twenty	Great Barrington to Bledington	179
Day Twenty-one	Bledington to Moreton-in-Marsh	190

THE MAKING OF OXFORDSHIRE

The irregular shape of Oxfordshire demands some historical explanation. Other parts of England were divided into shires before Oxfordshire was thought of! Wessex, an ancient kingdom of the west Saxons was a shire in the eighth century AD. The great Midland kingdom of Mercia was divided into shires after the Danish invasions and after the English had successfully reconquered the Danelaw in the tenth century. Oxfordshire was on the shifting boundary between Wessex and Mercia. Throughout the eighth century it was a sort of no-man's land between these two major power blocs. The city of Oxford originated as a 'burh' or fortified place to defend the Thames crossing against the Danes and was mentioned as such in the Anglo Saxon chronicle of 912 AD. In the tenth century the hinterland to the north was used as a recruiting ground and an area to maintain them for the garrison defending the burh and the surrounding countryside.

This area consisted of between 1300 and 1500 'hides', units of land which each supported one soldier who defended a four to five foot length of rampart of the 'burh' or fortified place (examples being Oxford and Wallingford). By the time the Normans carried out the survey of national resources known as Domesday Book (1086) Oxfordshire had 2400 hides. By this time the shire system had developed beyond a purely military arrangement; it had administrative and judicial functions. The king's representative the sheriff (Shire Reeve) held the shire court annually in the county town thus administering royal justice and protecting royal interests. The shire continued to be the principal unit of local administration and law for seven hundred years.

The irregularities of the county boundary can be explained as it followed pre-existing boundaries whether these were Iron Age, Roman, Saxon or Medieval, lay or ecclesiastical. The shire system was, in fact, imposed on a landscape already densely settled and mostly cultivated and already divided up. The sure indication of this is seen in the indented course followed for four miles between Upper Wardington and the northernmost tip of the county, the so-called Three Shires Stone. The boundary is here following the right angles of furlong blocks of early field systems. In the south western part the boundary is a good deal more curving and smoother; since the limestone uplands of the Cotswold hills were mainly sheep pastures and did not have so much of the land under arable cultivation. The strange shape of Chastleton is explicable as an Iron Age estate based on the fort in the middle of the parish.

In the 17th, 18th and 19th centuries, it was even more ragged and contained isolated portions of other counties. In the north west there were enclaves of Worcestershire, formerly parts of the estates of the bishops of Worcester. This explains the 'Four Shire Stone' at the junction of parts of Oxfordshire, Gloucestershire, Warwickshire and Worcestershire.

The one long stretch of Oxfordshire boundary determined by a major geographical feature was the southern, the line of the river Thames, a useful barrier in case of Mercian or Danish invasion of the kingdom of Wessex whose heartland lay to the south.

The most extensive modern redrafting of the boundary occurred in 1974 when the whole of the Vale of the White Horse and a strip of adjoining downland parishes were incorporated in the enlarged Oxfordshire in order to even out population figures between the densely peopled Berkshire and the thinly settled Oxfordshire.

Now, the boundary is marked in several different ways. A hedgerow, generally higher and less managed, and often containing a rich mix of flowering shrub species indicating great age is one sign. This is often backed up with a ditch, ditches and/or linear mounds. Sometimes the boundary is marked by long and sinuous green lane, lined with elderly hedgerows. In other places it follows the wriggling course of a brook or the straightened course of a watery drain. Some bridges have inscribed stones (as at Ickford) or plaques calling attention to the fact that two county authorities were involved in the construction or repair. Only very occasionally does the boundary follow a metalled road. Where several counties came together there might be an inscribed stone marking the point, as at the Four Shire Stone in the north west of the county.

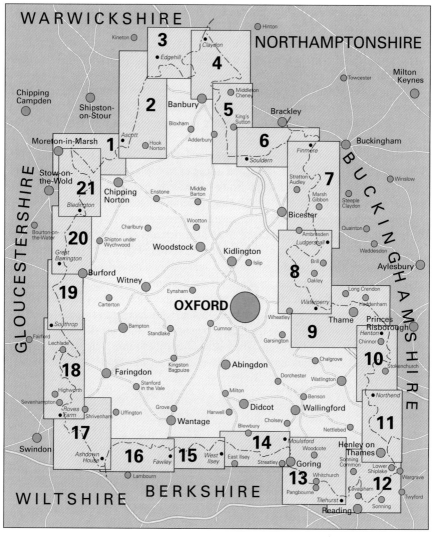
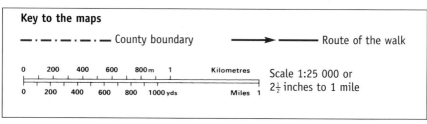

Day One

Moreton-in-Marsh to Ascott

Moreton-in-Marsh GR 213324 to Ascott GR 322347

Our first day starts by walking within three shires — from Gloucestershire to Warwickshire and into Oxfordshire. We follow the Rollright ridge along a former saltway with wide views north, pass an ancient stone circle and discover carvings of Norman beakheads and Jonah being swallowed by a very thin whale!

Distance: 11.3 miles (18.7 km).

Maps: Outdoor Leisure 45 – The Cotswolds.
Explorer 191 – Banbury, Bicester and Chipping Norton.
Landranger 151 – Stratford-upon-Avon and surrounding area.

Transport: Great Western/Thames Trains – London/Oxford/Hereford/
Worcester/Birmingham.
National Rail enquiries – Tel: 0845 7484950.

Taxis: Moreton-in-Marsh • Cotswolds Taxis – Tel: 07710 117471.
• Town and Country Taxis – Tel: 01608 674477.
Chipping Norton • Door to Door Taxis – Tel: 0973 892473.
• Snipp's Taxis – Tel: 01608 643049.

Car Parking: Moreton-in-Marsh – in the minor roads of the housing estate north of the A44 (GR 213324) on the eastern edge of the town.
Ascott – on the wide grass verge in the village near the entrance of the narrow lane from the south.

Accommodation/Public Houses/Refreshments:
Moreton-in-Marsh • Four Shires B&B – Tel: 01608 615412.
• Acacia B&B – Tel: 01608 650130.
• Treetops – Tel: 01608 651036.
• Warwick House Guest House – Tel: 01608 650773.

1

Great Wolford	• Lower Barn Farm – Tel: 01608 674435.
	• Manor Farm – Tel: 01608 651036.
Long Compton (1.5 miles from route)	
	• Ashby House – Tel: 01608 684286.
	• Butlers Road Farm – Tel: 01608 684262.
	• Tallet Barn – Tel: 01608 684248.
Great Rollright	• Hutton Grange – Tel: 01608 737339.
	• Wyatt Tea Rooms – Tel: 01608 684835.
	10am–5pm (summer) 10am–4.30pm (winter).
	Lunches available and farm produce sold.
Ascott	• Ascott House Farm – Tel: 01608 684655.
Whichford (0.5 miles from Ascott)	
	• Horseshoe Cottage – Tel: 01608 684310.
	• Norman Knight PH (meals) – Tel: 01608 684621.

For full accommodation lists, apply to Cotswold District Council Offices, High Street, Moreton-in-Marsh, GL56 0AZ – Tel: 01608 650881 or Chipping Norton Tourist Information Centre – Tel: 01608 644379.

The origin of the name **Moreton-in-Marsh**, refers to a farmstead and 'in Marsh' is a corruption of the *Hennemerse* or 'place frequented by wild birds', such as moorhens. The town stands on the great Roman road, the Fosse Way (now the A429).

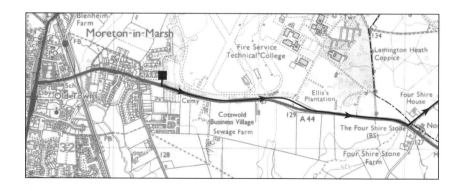

Walk east from the town on the northern verge of the A44 for 1.1 miles past the Fire Service Technical College, to the Four Shire Stone (GR 230322) at the junction of the minor road to Great Wolford.

The Four Shire Stone – why four?
Although there are only three shires that meet at the stone today, Oxfordshire, Warwickshire and Gloucestershire, detached parts of Worcestershire joined at this place from 1017 until 1931.
The present stone was built in the same style as other buildings on the Great Wolford estate.
Margaret Shepard, a local resident, describes how, over the years, the Four Shire Stone became the haunt of vagabonds. Prizefighting and other illegal sports took place there, since, if pursued by the constables of one county, it was easy to slip into the next one, and the next, and so on!

At this formal start of the walk, there is an ideally situated Four Shires B&B. Leave Gloucestershire to enter **Warwickshire** (our second shire) by taking the road towards Great Wolford for 750 yards. Turn right (E) at GR 236326 into a small paddock where there is a fenced grave of a young local farmer. Cross the stile and keep on the right side of the hedgerow, over a stile at the end of the first field, and through a gap in the hedge at the end of the second field. Continue along this hedge to a triangular coppice. As you walk, you will see an ancient antlered oak (probably 150 years old) and sawn-off stumps of diseased elm among other hedgerow species. At the coppice,

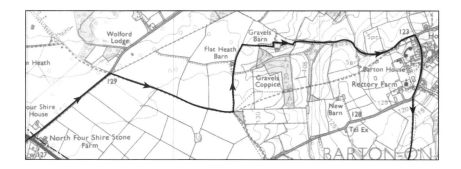

the footpath has been diverted, so turn left to walk north on the left side of a hedge with large oak trees. At the end of this path, pass Flat Heath Barn to the left, then turn right onto a track between deer paddocks, passing Gravels Barn. Walk east past a pond to ascend the track to **Barton-on-the-Heath**.

At the crossroads, turn right (signposted Little Compton) to Barton-on-the-Heath triangular village green. There is a fine well-house dated 1918, built as a memorial to the elder son of Major and Mrs Bird. The houses are built of ironstone, the iron oxide in the soil colouring the ploughed fields a vivid orangey-rust colour. Barton House is an early 17th century Cotswold house with characteristic triple chimneys, gables and ball finials.

Access point: Barton-on-the-Heath, 3.1 miles. Please take care not to obstruct the narrow roads. Telephone box . GR 257326.

Follow the sign to Moreton. St Lawrence's church is worth a diversion. The building is late Norman; in his book *'The buildings of England – Warwickshire'*, Pevsner states that 'there was probably an Anglo-Danish church here; for one North chancel window has a remodelled head of the early 11th century with a loose interlace and a serpent'. Certainly the Norman chancel arch has a carving of what looks like a wild boar on the east side, reflecting that this land was originally wild heathland and forest. There is a fine brass of an Elizabethan merchant. The modern turquoise, red, yellow and blue stained glass glows brightly in contrast to the ancient medieval glass. There are the remains of a holy-water stoup (basin) as well as small areas of ancient painting. The saddleback roof of the tower is unusual. We particularly liked the blacksmith's (1986) work of animals and birds on the church gates and the wheel design near the bus stop.

One hundred yards past the road junction near the church, branch left over a stile at the bend in the road. Go downhill (S 185°) bearing slightly right over the ridge and furrow (the evidence of medieval ploughing) to cross through the gap in the hedge. In this first field, *do not* bear further west to the new stile in the right-hand field hedge. In the next field, bear further right (W) to the small oak tree at the corner of the field, the furthest right of the three hedgerow trees. Go over the stile and keep in the same direction on the right side of the hedge while climbing gently up the Rollright ridge. Continue by the hedge alongside two fields, then after 30 yards in the third one, turn left over a stile erected by the Cotswold Voluntary Wardens Service. Go up the hill, climbing more steeply, keeping the clump of larch trees to your right (167°), over a stile and through the left gateway. Keep straight ahead with the hedge on your right. Climb over the small stile in the wire fence, and continue up the side of the field along the left side of a wooden fence. Follow the grassy track to Salters Well Farm. This is an interesting name, probably dating from the days of transportation of salt on the Droitwich Saltway that ran east from Worcestershire towards Great Rollright. From Iron Age and Roman times, salt was produced as a vital commodity for food preservation and the Anglo-Saxons developed an extensive, well organised network of saltways.

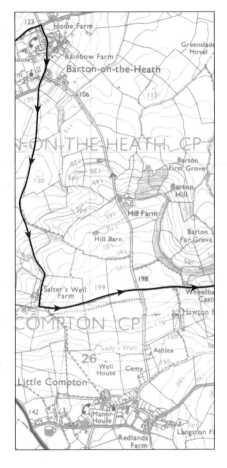

Turn sharp left after Salters Well Farm to join the bridleway (the former saltway) along the ridge. Look out in late summer for comma and red admiral butterflies on the nettles and flowers beside the path. Along this section there may be splendid views south to Little Compton manor house and north-east to Long Compton church. Cross the minor road and continue past a house near Wheelbarrow Castle (origin of name not known) to the deserted farm buildings at Neakings.

Keep on in the same direction (*do not* turn left here), through the steel gate, and gently uphill with the hedgerow to your right. On the approach to the second field where the slope flattens, note the thick, twisting hedge coming up the hill to the right. This is a triangular 'point' of Oxfordshire poking into Warwickshire. The footpath has been diverted here; therefore, at the hedge at the far end of the second field up the slope, continue left along the bridleway and follow it round at the top of the hill towards the radio mast. Emerge onto the road and bear left along the road (SE 110°) towards **Little Rollright**.

Access point: Entry of bridleway onto Little Compton/Little Rollright road, 5.6 miles. GR 280308.

In autumn you may find the shaggy ink cap (or lawyer's wig) toadstools in this area. Many people consider these among the most delicious of any toadstool. The county boundary hedgerow on the right side of the road is about 30 feet wide in places with a 15-foot-wide bank. There are some very ancient, coppiced ash trees. The

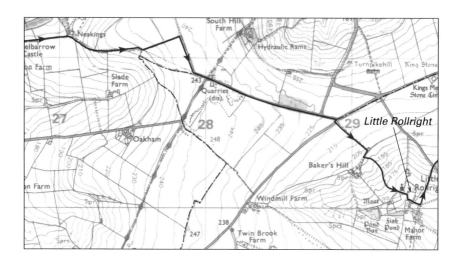

trunks, which are likely to be 300–400 years old, are multiple trunks and have sprung up from ground stools (roots). There are also patches of primitive ferns, an indicator of ancient woodland. The fact that the county boundary follows the road is a clue that the road existed before the boundary. Walk for just over 0.5 miles along this road with a view of Long Compton to the left. Pass by a minor road joining from the left on to a T-junction.

Option to see the Rollright Stones (750 yards east)

Walk left along the road (the county boundary), past the house called the Toll House (indicating that this road was once a turnpike road), to the Rollright Stones. These are a Bronze Age stone circle situated to the south of the road. To the north is an outlier, the King Stone, eight feet high. Pevsner suggests that: 'This outlier is almost certainly directional and served as a marker to guide people to the stone circle itself'.

Cross the road at the T-junction and enter a wide stony farm track through a white steel-barred gate and walk into **Oxfordshire**, our third shire, for the first time. Descend towards the village of **Little Rollright**, pass a concrete barn, and continue by bearing left off the track and onto a footpath down the hill directly towards Little Rollright church. Pevsner in *'The buildings of England – Oxfordshire'*, describes this church as 'informal and homely'. Inside there are two large tomb chests of members of the Dixon family in alabaster and black marble.

The Rollright Stones

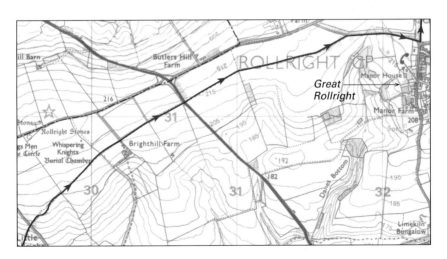

   Walk down the road past the Old Rectory. There is a reset 13th century window in the barn wall on the corner. Just as you leave the hamlet and at the start of a wall on your right, turn sharp left (NE) up the grassy bank behind the hedge on the left. Climb up the hillside (029°) along the route of the D'Arcy Dalton Way (a long-distance footpath from Wormleighton in Warwickshire to Wayland's Smithy in south Oxfordshire), to cross a small lane, and go through a steel gate. Follow the footpath (which formerly was beside a stone wall) across the next field. Towards the end of this second field, look left. About 150 yards away is a Neolithic portal dolmen or burial chamber called The Whispering Knights (see below). The pine trees surrounding the Rollright Stones can be seen further uphill to the left. A folk tale about these stones runs as follows:

The king and the witch

A legendary king at the head of his army was advancing up the hill, from which Long Compton could be seen. Just as he neared the top, a witch who owned the ground appeared and said,

> 'Seven long strides shalt thou take;
> If Long Compton thou canst see,
> King of England thou shalt be.'

Exulting, the king cried out,

> 'Stick, stock, stone,
> As King of England I shall be known,'

and strode forward, but instead of Long Compton, a long earthern mound rose up before him and the witch shrieked in reply,

> 'Rise up, stick, and stand still, stone,
> For King of England thou shalt be none;
> Thou and thy men hoar stones shall be
> And I myself an eldern tree.'

The King became a single stone (the King Stone) and his men a circle (the Rollright Circle). The stones of the burial chamber (the Whispering Knights) are said to be traitors who, when the King was about to fight the enemy, drew themselves apart and were plotting treason when they were turned into stone by the witch.

Go over two stiles, cross a farm track, go through the next two fields towards the busy A3400 road and bear left through the thick roadside hedge. Turn right to walk on the road verge for approximately 20 yards. Cross with care, and climb the concrete steps on the other roadside bank. Walk away from the road (064°) along the line of a former hedgerow for two fields. The buildings of **Great Rollright** village can be seen ahead. Follow the hedgerow onto a track (with a thin strip of woodland to the right) towards some wooden gates. At the road walk right to the crossroads at the north end of Great Rollright. Should you wish to visit the **Wyatt Tea Rooms**, walk left along the minor road for 450 yards. For details see 'Refreshments' above.

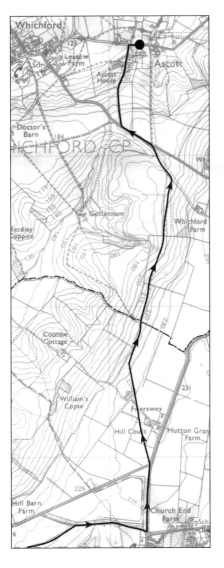

Access point: Wide verge near the crossroads north of Great Rollright, 8.8 miles. Shop, post office and telephone. GR 322315.

Great Rollright church is well worth a visit. From the crossroads, walk east for 0.25 miles along the road sign-posted 'Hook Norton'. Outside the church, the Norman doorway has an arch with a band of beakheads showing the Scandinavian influence in the architecture; a carving of Jonah being spat out by a very slim whale; and outside, some beautifully carved heads of people who may have been contributors to the church in 1450. Lozenges of grisaille glass (13th century) are easy to spot as they look 'gravelly' from the exterior where the surface of the glass has become weather-worn. Inside, there is a carved rood screen and ancient glass.

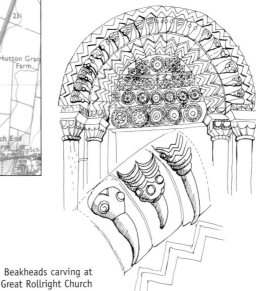

Beakheads carving at
Great Rollright Church

Return to the crossroads and leave Great Rollright by turning right (N) along the road to Whichford (*not* the bridleway), past an impressive stand of beech trees on the left and a decaying stone wall on the right. Hutton Grange (B&B) is reached within 0.5 miles (N). Where our route meets a road from the left, climb over the metal five-barred gate and follow the footpath (NW 352°) to a stile, and into the next field. At the next stile cross the farm track, climb over the next stile, and then aim (354°) for the gap between the right (N) of the farm buildings and the end of the hedge.

Walk diagonally right downhill (NW 350°) towards the ash tree in the field below. On reaching the fence and the remains of another hedge, turn right to walk along the uphill side of the fence to the end of the field and cross over the stile. The hedgerow growing up and over the brow of the hill is the county boundary. It is characteristically twisting, with standard trees and is multi-specied. We are now back in **Warwickshire**. The hedge of the next field (which the footpath used to follow) has been removed so continue straight on by keeping to the contours of the slope (020°) and aiming left of the solitary electric pole in the field, to the metal five-barred gate beyond it. The next field is grassy and 'lumpy', a possible site of former quarrying. Keep straight ahead and slightly downhill (018°). Climb the stile at the waymark in the hedge, left of an old ash tree. Walk through this field, keeping along the hedge to your left, and through the next field. Pass through a hole in the hedge just uphill from the field corner and over a stile. Turn left to follow the hedge down a grassy track towards a metal gate. Just before the gate, turn right to cross a stile in the hedge onto the road.

The footpath from here to **Ascott** is currently under review, so we recommend taking the quiet lanes' option. Therefore, turn left at the road, and then turn first right down a narrow lane towards the hamlet of Ascott (B&B at Ascott House Farm). At the next junction, turn right for the car parking venue on the road verges.

Day Two

Ascott to Edgehill

Ascott GR 322347 to Edgehill GR 375472

A day walking, in part actually on the county boundary along Ditchedge Lane, with wide views west across Warwickshire. It is ironstone country and the houses and fields are a deep orangey-rust colour. The day ends with a high level walk along the scarp of Edgehill, above the site of the indecisive Royalist battle in 1642.

Distance: 10.7 miles (17 km).

Maps: Explorer 191 – Banbury, Bicester and Chipping Norton.
                 Explorer 206 – Edge Hill and Fenny Compton.
                 Landranger 151 – Stratford-upon-Avon and surrounding area.

Taxis: Banbury   • ABC Taxis – Tel: 01295 258888/268888.
                              • Banbury Taxis – Tel: 01295 263838/267878.

Car Parking: Ascott – on the wide grass verge in the village near the entrance of the narrow lane from the south.
               Edgehill – on the grass verge of minor road south-east of the village.

Accommodation/Public Houses/Refreshments:

Epwell	• Chandler's Arms – Tel: 01295 780344.
	• Yarnhill Farm (0.8 miles from route) – Tel: 01295780250.
Upper Tysoe	• Laurel House, Shipston Road – Tel: 01295 588285.
Middle Tysoe	• Brookland B&B, Peacock Lane – Tel: 01295 680202.
	• Peacock Inn – Tel: 01295 680338.
Edgehill	• Castle Inn B&B – Tel: 01295 670255.
	• Upton House Tea Room – Tel: 012956 70266.
Ratley	• Rose and Crown B&B – Tel: 01295 678148.

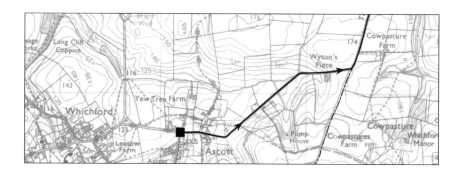

From the centre of **Ascott**, walk uphill towards **Sibford Gower** (E, then NE) past Vernon House on the right, and along the minor road to meet the county boundary south of Cowpasture Farm. Turn left at the junction and continue north for 1 mile along Traitor's Ford Lane, a broad grass-verged road with ancient ash trees marking the boundary as described on Day 1. Continue north in the direction of Lower Brailes to Traitor's Ford, through the infant River Stour. The origin of the name 'Traitor's Ford' is a mystery; it has had this name since 1807 with no explanation! The river flows from east to west which means that it will eventually join the River Severn: we are therefore on the western edge of the watershed of the Cotswold Hills.

Immediately after crossing the ford by the footbridge, bear right onto a bridleway leading uphill along Ditchedge Lane. This green lane is the county boundary, also with ancient ash trees and stumps of diseased elms. It is straight, with bracken growing along the right verge. Sibford Gower can be seen in the valley to the right. Walk for 1.75 miles along this ancient way. Here we follow the Macmillan Way, a path from Boston in Lincolnshire to Chesil Beach in Dorset. Turn right where Ditchedge Lane meets the road from Swalcliffe to Lower Brailes, to continue north, with care, on the road for 230 yards, then bear left to keep due north where the road bears right. Enter a green lane, called Beggars Lane, which is one of the most ecologically diverse pieces of the county boundary encountered so far, with ancient ashes, old coppiced hazel, sycamores, field maple, decaying elm tree stumps and oak. The air was full of birdsong when we walked through. There are views to the Cotswold Hills (SW) and to the Malvern Hills (W), with the villages of Stourton and Upper Brailes in the foreground.

Continue north past the mast and wooden buildings. After 80 yards, cross a small stile hidden in the hedge on the right. Walk east (072°) across a field to a steel five-barred gate on the left side of a small coppice. The soil is very fine, of Lower Estuarine series. Field pansies, scarlet pimpernel and common speedwell were in flower as we passed in late October. At the gate, turn right into the lane, then almost immediately left (NE), continuing downhill towards **Epwell**. Turn right along the far

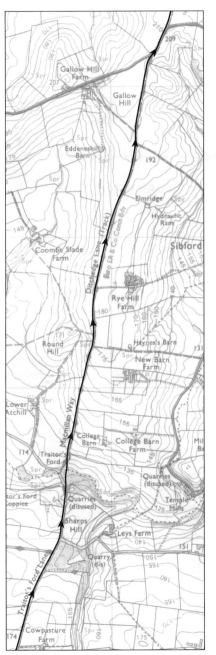

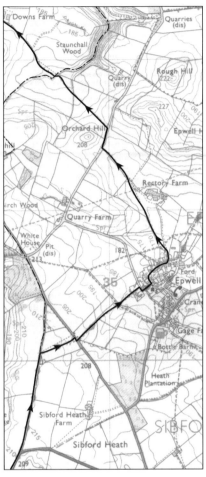

edge of the second field, then immediately left, and follow the path onto the village street and turn right towards the church. Should you wish to divert to the Chandlers Arms with its massive beams, then keep right (SE) along the footpath of the second field edge.

The well giving Epwell its name is on the roadside verge 100 yards north-east of the Chandlers Arms. The church is situated on a small hill above the street and is of mainly 18th century architecture being built of a ginger-coloured (iron-impregnated) shelly sandstone. Many of the village houses are of the same stone: some are thatched and the steep pitch of other roofs betray the fact that they had previously been thatched. The roofs had to be steeply pitched for the rain to fall off quickly.

Access point: Epwell, 4.5 miles. Telephone, pub. GR 353405.

To continue, pass the church on your right, and turn left at the churchyard corner along the back lane which curves right. After 200 yards, turn left (N) along the *second* marked footpath immediately beyond Rose Cottage and before Rectory Farm. Bear left (NW) across the first field. *Do not* go over the stone-walled bridge on the track, instead, find a stile in the hedgerow. Cross the wooden footbridge over the small brook and bear diagonally left (NW 338°) along the right side of an ancient hedge full of crab apple trees. Yarn Hill, a conical hill covered with gorse and bracken, can be seen to the east. Keep to the same direction as the first part of the hedgeline where it bears left after a short distance and cross the field passing left (W) of Rectory Farm. Keep left of a pylon to a stile onto a farm track. Turn left. There are some good examples of ridge and furrow in the field on your left. Walk along this track (NW) to the road in front of Orchard Hill. Turn right (N) at the road and after 180 yards turn

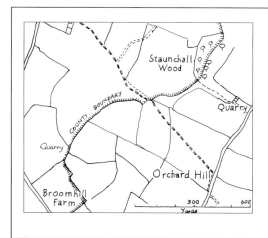

The Parliamentary Enclosure movement took place from about 1750–1850 over the Midlands and southern England and resulted in the open fields being replaced by a network of smaller hedged fields. The hedgerows are straight and have only two or three species.

Enclosure fields NW of Epwell

left (NW) onto a farm track to Downs Farm. At the end of the first field, bear right (NW 328°) and cross the field to a small wooden gate and footbridge in the corner of a field in the county boundary hedgeline. This hedge is wide and twisting compared to the straight, narrow enclosure hedge that we have just passed through. The county boundary also has a ditch and a much richer plant life which attracts more diverse species of birds. We saw goldfinches feeding on the thistle seed beside the boundary.

Go through a wooden gate and cross the stream into **Warwickshire**, then turn left with the stream on your left. *Do not go through the metal gates, instead turn right (NW) up the hill on right-hand side of hedge along the cart track to Downs Farm.* Go through the yard and down the track to the road. Turn right and walk down the road for 180 yards, to where a plank and stile cross the thick hedgerow on the right side of the road. In the field, walk half-left down it (N 354°) or keep your eye on the red pantiles of Rose Farm in **Upper Tysoe** below, once this is visible over the brow of the hill. If you look left, you will see the windmill above

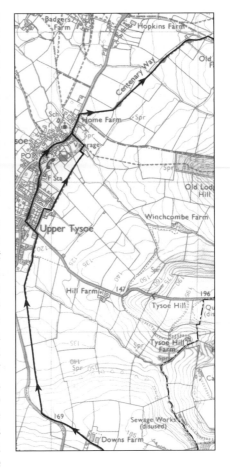

the Tudor manor house of Compton Wynyates. Aim for the stile to the left of the lone ash tree in the first hedgerow, then down the next field to cross the bridge over the brook in front of Rose Farm. Walk behind the houses of Upper Tysoe keeping Rose Farm on your left. Continue north, over a stile in the corner, to walk along a narrow path between fields. Go over a stile onto a path behind the house gardens and beside allotments, and through a wooden gate onto the road. Turn left here to the main village street. *See Alternative route below.*

At the village street turn right (N) to go through the village, where there are some good examples of thatched ironstone cottages. There are several biblical quotes in plaques on the walls on the left and by the horse trough. For those with geological interest, in the walls of the building opposite L.J. Carter's (the family butcher), there are streaks of iron ore as well as fossilised shells in the crumbly ironstone.

Access Point: Middle Tysoe, 7.5 miles. Shops, post office, telephone, pub. GR 339442.

Alternative route

If you are particularly interested to see a fine example of the reverse 'S' bend pattern remains of medieval ploughing in a field of ridge and furrow, then, near the gate leading out of the allotments, turn right along Middleton Close, then right again along Welchman Place, then left before the wall of a white-painted garage and continue along on the left-hand edge of a football pitch. Climb over another stile; the ridge and furrow field is on the right side of the path.

The reversed "S' bend pattern of ridge and furrow ploughing

Rejoin the main route by continuing north, then turn left over a stile into a small paddock, then right to keep to the left-hand edge of a small wood. Cross over the stile in the right-hand corner, and cross another field in the direction of white wrought-iron gates. *Do not* go through these gates, but turn sharp left and through a steel five-barred gate into a narrow lane; at the second iron gate turn right between the gardens, keeping the brick garden wall to the right. Peacock Lane is at the end of this path. Turn left into the lane to join the main road and meet the route near the church.

The shape of ridge and furrow is determined firstly, by the length that the eight-oxen plough team could reach before needing a rest (220 yards), and secondly by the width (11 yards) imposed by the restrictions of the half-acre strips within the open field system. The reversed S-bend or wave-like pattern was produced by the ploughman who needed to begin to turn his somewhat cumbersome team well before reaching the headland at the end of the strip.

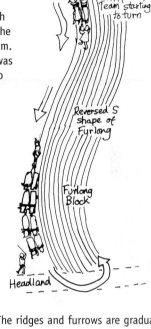

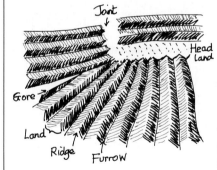

How ridge and furrow is formed

The ridges and furrows are gradually formed over time by the soil being shifted by the plough up the slope of the infant ridge, and of digging further into the furrow.

Middle Tysoe church is worth a diversion, partly to see the clerestory (part of the church wall above the aisle roof which has a series of windows), but mainly to see how a church looks when the plaster is removed, as was done in Victorian times. Of interest too, is a stone effigy of William Clarke in Elizabethan dress. It shows his costume well, with its cap, ruff, buttoned doublet and hose. In the churchyard there is a preaching cross.

Continue along the main road to the edge of the village, pass Home Farm on the right, then turn right (E) over a stile, then diagonally half-left (080°) across a field (*not* along the track) to the protruding field corner. Here is a sign marking the

Centenary Way, a long-distance footpath from Kingsbury, east of Sutton Coldfield, to Meon Hill in Warwickshire, with the Warwickshire symbol of the bear and ragged staff, originally the heraldic insignia of the Earl of Warwick. Keep along the hedge boundary of this first L-shaped field, then bear slightly right at the end to go through a wide gap in the hedge at the end of the field. Continue along the field edges of four small fields. Before the barns, bear diagonally right (089°) across the field and over a stile in the far corner. Turn right to go directly uphill by the hedge, through the gate and bear left (084°) away from Old Lodge Farm situated on the hillside. Follow the route of an ancient ditch between the ridge and furrow up towards the wooded

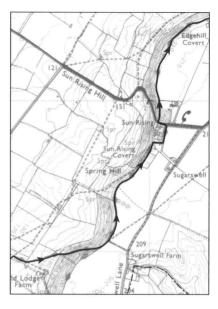

scarp slope. Take the left of the two gates into the wood and follow the bridleway diagonally up the slope through the wood. At the top, on the watershed of the Cotswolds, turn left (N) along the footpath. A dreary winter's day was enlivened for us by watching a party of crossbills, birds that are a regular but uncommon visitor from Scandinavia. They were dextrously splitting the larch cones with their strong bills.

On the footpath keep to the contours for 270 yards to reach Spring Hill, the marlstone scarp edge with its wide views. The land below is known as the Vale of the Red Horse, the name reflecting the red of the iron-stone soil. From here, you can see the Malvern Hills (W), the Clee Hills (NW) and the gasometers on the outskirts of Coventry. The long, linear grassy mounds (NW) are roofs of munitions stores and the white, modern buildings (N) are the Rover Research Development Unit at Gaydon.

Crossbills

Keep to this path which diverts to the right side of Sun Rising House, cross the A422 road (with care!) and continue through a grove of laurels. Keep on the uphill side of the woods through which, in winter when the trees are bare, the beginnings of the Vale of Evesham can be seen. Among the many tree fungi we saw, was *Auricularia auricula-judae* (commonly known as Jew's Ear) on the dead elder branches.

There is now 1.4 miles of woodland walking.

Should you wish to shorten the route, it is possible to turn sharp right (SE) uphill at King Johns Lane (see below) to then follow the minor road into Edgehill.

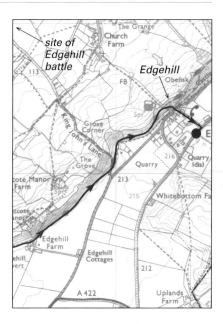

After 0.3 miles along the scarp edge, Edgehill Farm is reached. Here, take the minor road downhill for 30 yards, go through the gate pillars, then turn up the slope to continue on the path at the top of the escarpment. Edgehill is aptly named: below you is a very steep scarp slope and the cliffs of marlstone rock (a Jurassic limestone) can be seen as you leave Edgehill Farm. Continue for another 0.7 miles to meet King John's Lane. This is a sunken lane – sunken due to the many years of driving stock and waggons up and down this track. Our path keeps uphill past a more contemporary landmark, a fine beech tree with 'Hell's Angels' carved in its bark – presumably 30 years ago. Walk down King John's Lane for only 30 yards, then turn right up into the wood by some wooden steps and walk for another 0.4 miles to arrive at some steel railings. By going downhill and over the stile, you are able to see the obelisk (hidden in the lime trees to your right) commemorating the Battle of Waterloo. From this vantage point, it is possible to see the setting of the Battle of Edgehill in 1642. The site of the encounter was at Graveground Coppice 1.5 miles north-west of **Radway** GR 354492. There is a wonderful view west across Warwickshire.

The Battle of Edgehill, Sunday 23rd October 1642
As King Charles I was attempting to reach London to overthrow Parliament at the beginning of the Civil War, he was opposed by the Parliamentarian army under the command of the Earl of Essex at Edgehill. Although the King's cavalry and army numbered more than the Earl's 2,500 horses and 12,500 foot soldiers, it was an indecisive battle. 1,500 men died. This battle was the first and last chance that Charles had to overthrow Parliament. (For a vivid description of the battle, see D. Eddershaw, *The Civil War in Oxfordshire*, 1995.)

Retrace your steps to climb the scarp slopes using the steps by the steel railings. You arrive at Castle Inn. The Castle Inn tower has an interesting history. The architect Sanderson Miller (1716–1780), who lived at Radway Grange (GR 370480), reputedly built this octagonal Gothic tower as one of his first experiments in building. He used to gallop across with his guests from the grange below to use the tower as his dining room, which commanded a splendid view. He also designed the picturesque Gothic thatched cottage on Edgehill village street, just to the left of the tower. These were pioneer buildings of their kind, considered at the time more beautiful than anything by William Kent.

Cross the road, turn left (NE) for a few yards, then just before the post-box and a notice board for Ratley and Upton Parish Council, turn right into a narrow alley leading between the houses and away from the village on a raised way. Quarrying on either side of the public footpath has resulted in this curious feature. At another minor road, turn right to find suitable car parking on the grass verge. Accommodation is available at Ratley 0.6 miles further on (Day 3).

One mile south of Ratley, is the 15th century **Upton House** (GR370457) built of lemon-coloured Cotswold stone. It contains an outstanding collection of art, porcelain, tapestries and furniture. The garden is beautiful, with terraces leading down to a water-garden. Open April–October, Sat–Wed, 2–6pm, NT owned.

Day Three

EDGEHILL TO CLAYDON

Edgehill GR 375472 to Claydon GR 457500

A day travelling east, then north to our destination, to be near to where three shires — Oxfordshire, Warwickshire and Northamptonshire — meet at the northern tip of Oxfordshire. We see from the lynchets and ridge and furrow that medieval farmers ploughed this land, and there is an opportunity to date a hedge.

Distance: 10.2 miles (13.25 km).

Maps: Explorer 206 – Edge Hill and Fenny Compton.
Landranger 151 – Stratford-upon-Avon and surrounding area.

Taxis: Banbury   • ABC Taxis – Tel: 01295 258888/268888.
                       • Banbury Taxis – Tel: 01295 263838/267878.

Car Parking: Edgehill – on wide grass verge of minor road south-east of the village.
Claydon – north of the church by the telephone box, but please be careful not to obstruct the narrow roads.

Accommodation/Public Houses/Refreshments:

Ratley   • Rose and Crown Inn B&B – Tel: 01295 678148.
Horley (1.1 miles from route)
                       • Sor Brook House Farm B&B – Tel: 01295 738121.
Mollington   • Green Man PH – Tel: 01295 750692.
Farnborough   • Butchers Arms PH – Tel: 01295 690615.
Claydon   • Point to Point Farmhouse B&B – Tel: 01295 690346.
                       • Claydon House – Tel: 01295 690452. Coffees, lunches and teas.
                       • Bygones Museum – Tel: 01295 690258. Coffees, lunches and teas.

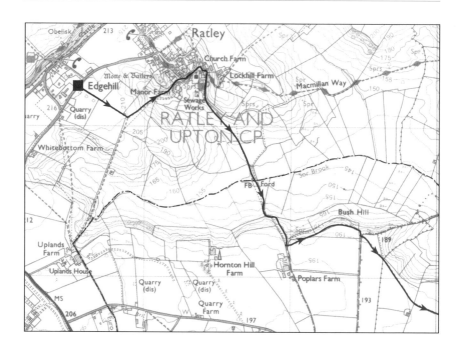

From the grass verge on the minor road on the edge of **Edgehill** village (GR 375472), walk south-east from the exit of the footpath ending Day 2 to take a footpath along a farm track to the left (SE 125°). Pass the barn on the left (the track turns right here) and turn left to climb over the stile. Bear right (NE 059°) along the narrow piece of field between the hedge and the barbed wire fence, downhill to the gate in the corner. **Ratley** church is visible and the remains of the motte and bailey castle of Ratley are in front of you. Walk on downhill, then after the second stile, continue along the grassy track and turn left to climb the right side of the castle mound. Walk on the path to the stile above the farm buildings of Manor Farm on the right. The origin of the name Ratley is 'cheerful clearing' from the Old English *rot* = cheerful. At the road, turn right towards the church. The cornice of an 1884 coach house on the right is worth examining. There are moulded images of an owl, a beehive, a shell, a cob of maize and a bunch of grapes in the tiles.

Ratley is within a conservation area and an Area of Outstanding Natural Beauty. The steep pitch of many of the roofs indicate that it, too, was originally a thatched village. Ratley churchyard has the crumbling remains of a preaching cross. The light and airy church is dedicated to St Peter ad Vincula (St Peter in Chains). It is built on the side of a steep slope and there are strong buttresses on the hillside wall to

THE FIRST
POST OFFICE
1882-1932

A land-girl's tale from 1947 about Ratley's first Post Office (1882–1932)
Just past the coach house is a cottage with its gable end facing the road. In the
wall is a horizontal slot: this was the former post-box and just at the height that
a little boy could reach. Inside the cottage, a stone shelf below the slot was used
for rice puddings to cool. The temptation to 'post' small stones was too great,
and the result was:

The boy not too tall hears his Mother call,
"Who coated our pudding with stones overall?"   Wendy Lines

support some of the weight of the building. Close to the church a natural spring provides pure water.

Pass the church and the Rose and Crown PH, to walk south (*not through the
entrance and footpath to Lockhill Farm*) by bearing right through an open gate along
a tarmac track past Featherbow House on the right. Continue on the ancient green
lane. *Do not* cross a stone stile in the wall on the right, but stay on the lane until it
turns left. Here, climb a wooden stile on the right, and walk (SE 162°) to a stile beside
a field gate, then across another field. Go through a small wooden gate to follow a
footpath between hedges with a small stream on the right. This path meets the larger
Sor Brook which marks the county boundary. This river boundary is accompanied by
a 20-foot-thick hedge, very rich in species, and twisting in contrast to the straight
hedges joining it.

Cross Sor Brook via the ford into **Oxfordshire**, and walk uphill through the newly planted wood. Go through a five-barred gate in the top corner of the field and continue on the start of an ancient 'sunken' way up the slope. Near the top a farm track joins from the left; turn sharp left (E 069°) along it and start descending for only 50 yards, then climb up the bank and bear right along the marked footpath, still on the same compass bearing. At the second footpath sign, keep parallel to the slope just below the curving hawthorn hedgerow at the top of Bush Hill, and not along by the wire fence. This path is also on part of the route of the d'Arcy Dalton Way.

We found a badger print showing the five toe claws pointing forwards, a flat oval mid-pad, and a smaller round pad at the back. Beware of the sett holes they have made in this area.

Just after a stile in a barbed wire fence, turn sharp right up the slope to the track above, then over two wooden stiles. Go diagonally left across the field (142°) continuing to climb gradually to the gap in the hedge; there, continue on in nearly the same direction (145°) to a stile in the next hedge boundary, left of an isolated stone field barn. A hedge starts here: continue along the left side of it (N 117°) to a stile into a paddock on the north side of Horley Fields Farm. Continue in the same direction by climbing over a stile and out of the paddock at the far end by another stile.

> Horley Fields is an isolated farm built in the 18th century when the Enclosure Act was passed. The layout is U-shaped with a double barn, one in old stone and the other is much more modern.

Continue along the downhill side of the hedge over a stile into the concrete-paved farmyard of Savee Farm. Continue ahead with high evergreen trees to the left and a large barn on the right. In the middle of a concreted yard, and at the gates below Glebe Farm, turn left down a concrete farm track for 140 yards. Cross through a steel gate on the right, then bear diagonally left (105°) across the field to a hedgerow corner by a brook. Continue by following the ditch, keeping it to the left (077°), then

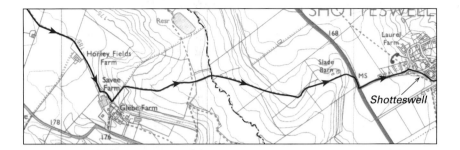

after 130 yards, bear right away from the ditch towards a stile in the hedge at the lower end of the field. Walk on east (065°) to cross the small footbridge over Sor Brook which still forms the county boundary.

Cross the boundary into **Warwickshire** over the footbridge, go uphill on the left side of the hedgerow for 30 yards, then turn right over a small wooden footbridge. Ascend the footpath across the hill (112°), go over a stile at the end of the first field and up across

Sor Brook is a tributary of the River Cherwell. Our route is now on the dip slope of the Cotswold escarpment with these rivers draining east into the Thames basin. This is in contrast to Day 2 when the brooks that we crossed at Traitor's Ford and at Upper Tysoe flow westwards, and are tributaries of the River Avon and the Severn Estuary.

the slope past the telegraph poles to a steel gate in the second hedgerow. Turn left along the hedge boundary, through another gate and up the hill past Slade Barn on the left. There are fine examples of lynchets (see page 26) in the steep slope to your right and good examples of ridge and furrow evidence to your left.

At the top of the grassy track is a stile onto the road. Turn right then first left along the road signed 'Shotteswell'. There is a fine milestone with a benchmark.

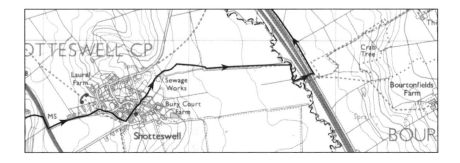

The Formation of Lynchets
The population increased in the early middle ages until the 13th century; land was short and the farmers began to cultivate the steep slopes in strips along the contours. Their oxen and ploughs cut into the hillside building up a series of terraces known as lynchets.

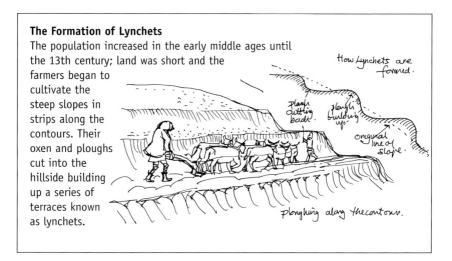

In **Shotteswell**, locally pronounced 'Satchell', turn right at the green with a bus shelter into which is incorporated an ancient mullioned window that needed a home! Go along Coronation Lane, keeping right at Middle Lane, then left down Chapel Lane. This route takes you past Shotteswell Church, which has a rich collection of church furnishings.

Shotteswell Church
By the door is a Norman font. The wooden screens are of medieval-aged oak as are the pulpit and pews. The stone seats to the left in the north aisle and at the back of the church, are the origin of the proverb 'Let the weakest go to the wall,' reminding us of the days when churches had no pews and everyone who could, remained standing. Also at the back of the church is a picture of George III with the royal coat of arms, comprising the lions of England and Scotland; the dragon of Wales and the harp of Ireland, supported by a lion and a unicorn, and the Hanoverian white horse in the centre. On the far external wall of the church is a scratch dial, a primitive clock to indicate the hours of mass.

Access Point: Shotteswell, 4.2 miles. Limited parking is possible in Coronation Lane. GR 426455.

On leaving the church, rejoin Chapel Lane and walk down into Middle Lane. Follow the road left to the beginning of Bakehouse Lane. Here, turn right. The more northerly and direct footpath to Mollington has been blocked by the construction of the M40 motorway. We rejoin the route of the d'Arcy Dalton Way for a mile. Walk along a raised bank (NE 036°) and skirt left of the sewage-works, then over a stile in the direction of the motorway (093°). Walk along the left (N) side of the hedge until reaching a stile and a sleeper bridge. Cross to the right side of the hedge, then continue to the large hedge before the motorway. Turn right and parallel to the motorway, then left over a footbridge across a brook which is the county boundary between Oxfordshire and Warwickshire. Cross the motorway via the concrete footbridge. Turn left along the wooden fence by the motorway and go through four fields to the end of a long linear wood and a signpost indicating the D'Arcy Dalton Way. Turn right away from the motorway and walk beside the wood towards the village of Mollington on the hill to the right. Walk along this path for *only* 60 yards from the motorway, then look for a hidden footpath through the linear wood and over a footbridge. Cross the field on the far side by walking diagonally right (032°) and aiming for the centre of the buildings of **Mollington** village. Go over a small wooden stile in the hedgerow at the end of this first field. Continue in the same direction to a gate in the left hedge, just before the opposite corner of the field. Go through it, turn right and walk keeping the hedge to the right to join an

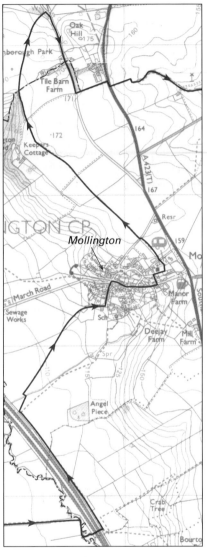

asphalt track. Turn right past the farmyard to the right and into Lower Farm Lane which leads up to the village street. Turn right at the telephone box and along the main village street, passing Chestnut Road on the right.

Access Point: Mollington, 6.7 miles. Parking in the village hall car park, at the end of Chestnut Road, on south side of main village street. GR 440472.

Mollington (place name origin – Moll's Farm) has a Norman church with a Saxon gravestone. The Green Man public house is towards the east end of the village on the main street beyond the church.

Leave Mollington by the steeply ascending Church Lane, which turns left from the village street just opposite the Garden House, and before reaching the public house. Go through the churchyard and out through a gate on its upper slope, northwards on the footpath through a garden, then along a path (NW) to a minor road. Cross the road and walk along the left side of a fence along a clearly defined path in the first field, then in the same direction (NW 317°) across two more fields, aiming for the centre of a wood and just right of a telegraph pole in the middle of the field. In winter, it is possible to see the top of the obelisk in the splendid gardens of **Farnborough Hall**. On reaching a track which crosses the road, continue along the footpath to the corner of the wood, cross the county boundary and walk diagonally right (NE 025°) to cross parkland (aim for Farnborough church spire) and join the road just left of a small lake.

Optional diversion of 550 yards north to Farnborough Hall, a classical stone house with an extensive garden and grand 0.7 mile terrace walk. N.T. owned. Open April–Sept, Wed & Sat 2-6 pm. Terrace only — Thurs & Fri 2-6 pm. Tel 01295 690202. No teas.

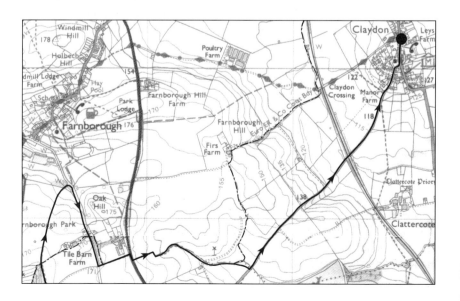

Turn sharp right (S) to walk along the road until the county boundary crosses the road at the entrance of Tile Farm. Continue walking for another 200 yards then turn sharp left (E) onto a footpath with the high, thick hedge on your left. This is the county boundary between Oxfordshire and Warwickshire and we estimated it to be 900 years old.

How to date a hedge — each species counts for a hundred years of age.

1. Take a sample length of 30 yards and count the number of flowering shrub species and trees.
2. Leave out brambles and woody climbers (eg ivy and honey-suckle).
3. Include alder, apple (including crab), ash, beech, blackthorn, briar, broom, buckthorn, cherry, dogwood, elder, elm, gorse, guelder rose, hawthorn, hazel, holly, hornbeam, lime, maple, oak, pine, plum, poplar, privet (wild), rowan, sallow, service tree, spindle, sycamore, wayfaring tree, whitebeam, willow and yew.
4. Count the species in 3 or more stretches, measured by taking 30 long strides (approximately 1 yard each), mark the length, then walk back to count the species. Calculate the average number of species per stretch.
5. Hedges with 2-3 species are likely to date from after the 18th century Enclosures Acts; those with 4–6 species are 16th–17th century, and those with 7–10 species are medieval. The oldest are likely to be parish or county boundary hedges.

Cross the busy A423 road by turning right, then almost immediately left. Cross the wide point-to-point track to the hedge leading away from the road, and walk along with the hedge on your left. Notice the irregular course of it: the ancient laid ash trees used as the hedge, the long linear mound and ditch, and the 'notching' (for explanation see Day 4). Pass on the left side of Point to Point farmhouse (B&B). At the farm, cross the race track again and maintain the same easterly direction by keeping the hedge and the Clattercote brook to the left. Emerge onto the minor road to the village of **Claydon**.

Turn left to walk north-east along the road, crossing under the railway bridge of the former Banbury–Warwick line to reach the village. It is worth looking at the 'telltales' on the inside of the railway bridge. These are small concrete blocks which indicate whether there is shift in the brickwork. They are dated 1987 and 1994. In some places there has been movement, so that part of the blocks have broken off.

Claydon (originally Clayey Hill) is the most northerly village in Oxfordshire. On the geological map (Banbury sheet 201) the Middle Lias is capped with a glacial deposit of boulder-clay. Claydon House, a beautiful late 18th century house, is passed on the left, and has stone *quoins* (French = corner) and keystones, a platband, and a shell portico above the door. The church, remarkable for its saddleback roof to the tower, is Norman in origin (there are transitional Norman arches and a squint). Inside, on the tablet describing the features of the church, is a reference to the Three Shires Stone. Although the text describes the stone as being in a field north of the church, there is now no sign of it at all, and its former position (GR 458525) is not on a public right of way This stone was at the northerly point of Oxfordshire, with Warwickshire to the west and Northamptonshire to the east.

The Bygones Museum near Claydon church includes a replica kitchen of the 1920s, local shops as they were, and steam and traction engines. Limited parking is available north of the telephone box.

Day Four

CLAYDON TO MIDDLETON CHENEY

Claydon GR 457500 to Middleton Cheney GR 500422 near The Red Lion public house in the High Street

We start our journey south along the eastern boundary of Oxfordshire. We cross into the fourth shire, Northamptonshire. In the church of Chacombe, someone in medieval times made fun of the Bishop, and at Middleton Cheney there are the beautiful colours and design of the William Morris and Burne–Jones windows.

Distance: 7.9 miles (12.6 km).

Maps: Explorer 206 – Edge Hill and Fenny Compton.
Landranger 151 – Stratford-upon-Avon and surrounding area.

Transport: London railway (Chiltern Line) – Oxford/Banbury/Kings Sutton/ Marylebone.
National Rail enquiries – Tel: 0845 7484950.

Taxis:
Banbury	• ABC Taxis – Tel: 01295 258888/268888.
	• Banbury Taxis – Tel: 01295 263838/267878.
King's Sutton	• Waverley Garage (Roger Moon) – Tel: 01295 811274.

Car Parking: Claydon – north of the church by the telephone box, but please be careful not to obstruct the narrow roads.
Middleton Cheney – High Street near Red Lion PH.

Accommodation/Public Houses/Refreshments:
Wardington (0.5 miles from route)	
	• Hare and Hounds PH – Tel: 01295 750645.
Upper Wardington	• Plough Inn – Tel: 01295 750476.
Chacombe	• George and Dragon Inn (B&B) – Tel: 01295 711500.
	• Berry Furze (B&B) – Tel: 01295 710145.
Middleton Cheney	• Red Lion PH – Tel: 01295 710978.
	• New Inn – Tel: 01295 710399.
	• Dolphin Inn – Tel: 01295 710314.
	• The Lodge (B&B) – Tel: 01295 710355.

From **Claydon** church take the village street lined by houses built of ironstone, bearing left (SE) in the direction of Cropredy. Where the road bends right, take the minor road straight ahead signposted 'Appletree and Chipping Warden' as far as the Oxford Canal. Instead of walking down the towpath leave the road over the stile beside a gate. Cross the field diagonally left (SE 145°) away from the canal to the footbridge in the field corner. Keeping the hedge on the right, continue south-east alongside two fields. In the field with a brick barn, continue beside the hedge, past a pond to where the hedge bends right. Here, bear diagonally left (SE 105°) to the far side. By an oak tree, go over a footbridge and cross a field aiming for the left side of a larch copse on the side of the hill. Walk up the slope along the county boundary between Oxfordshire and **Northamptonshire**, our fourth shire, and continue uphill on the left edge of the copse. Here the footpath has been diverted away from the footbridge and path leading through the wood, to circle left around the wood.

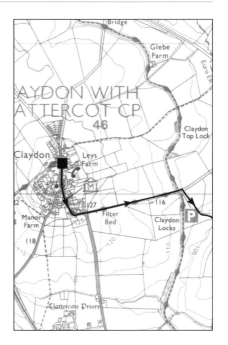

Go though the gate, turn left alongside the hedge, then right passing the footpath sign for the Macmillan Way to turn left (around the end of another ancient furlong block) and go through a gap in the hedge. Here, bear right (S 180°) downhill towards the point where the wood meets the minor road. Turn right along the road, then after one field, there is a gap in the hedge to the left. Go through this and cross the field by bearing half-left (SE 125°) towards the large willow trees at the point in the

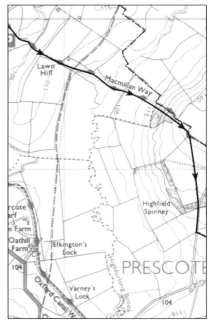

The County Boundary SE of Claydon

Before continuing through the gate at the top of the slope, turn to take a look back down the hill at the county boundary hedge below. At the end of the wood, there is a sharp turn right, then, only 100 yards further on, a sharp turn left. You can see on the map a number of these 'notches' in this area.

The reason for the 'notching' is because the county boundary was established after the open field farmers with their furlong blocks. Consequently, the boundary had to take into consideration the land division that already existed.

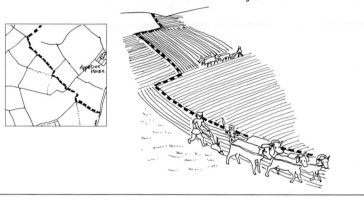

field where a brook crosses. Go over the footbridge and continue SE (156°) across a field. Then go along the right side of the hedge bordering the first part of the second field, before turning sharp right to follow a path crossing south-west (245°) towards Prescote Manor Farm.

This route avoids a dangerous road, the A361 from Hays Bridge into the village of Wardington. There are no footpaths or wide verges and there is fast traffic – not to be recommended!

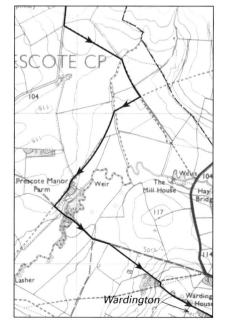

Walk across the field to a stile over the small brook marking the parish boundary. This is a fine hedge with mature trees. On the other side, bear left (SW 215°) across a field to a stile, then walk towards Prescote Manor Farm through another field to exit, just left of a small field barn, onto the farm track. Instead of walking alongside the farm buildings on the track, cross the track onto a footpath that runs 30 yards parallel to the right side of the farm. At the far hedge of this field turn sharp left at the footbridge onto a bridleway, cross the farm track again, and over a bridge spanning the infant River Cherwell, the source of which is in Northamptonshire. Follow the broad track through the wood, and beside the first two fields to the right. *Do not* take the first footpath right, instead continue to just after the hedge of the second field and take a footpath bearing right from the bridleway. There is a red-roofed barn on the far side of the field. Aim left of the barn (128°), go through the gap in the hedge and walk uphill along the left side of a small copse of coniferous trees. At the far corner of the copse, turn right across a plank bridge over the ditch, and along the narrow end of the wood, to turn left to follow the right side of a hedge continuing in a south-east direction (120°). Beware, *do not* take the wide path going to the right (W).

Go through the wooden gate at the end of the first field, then at the end of the second field, follow the footpath close to the left side of a large corrugated warehouse and down the drive in almost the same direction (135°) towards the

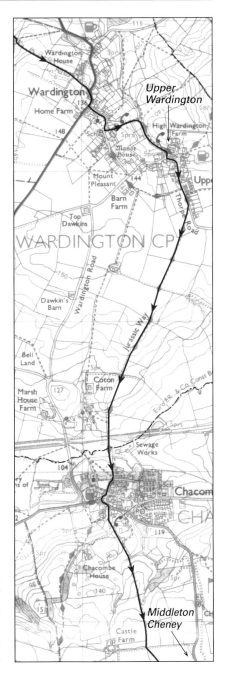

Steeply pitched roofs at Wardington, previously thatched

village of **Wardington**. On meeting the A361 Banbury to Daventry road, turn right, cross the road and go uphill. Turn left (SE) at the road junction signposted to Upper Wardington.

Access Point: Wardington Church, 4 miles. Limited car parking in the road leading to Upper Wardington. Telephone, post office and shop. GR 491463.

Wardington church has added aisles, hence its wide look. Here, as in Ratley (Day 3), the village house roofs are steeply pitched, so that the rain would run off quickly and not soak into the thatch. The chimneys have been heightened by using the blueish industrial bricks.

Go past the telephone box to leave Wardington by a footpath, keeping left of the triangular green, that leads east (073°) on a grassy track between stone walls. This is part of the Jurassic Way, a path from Stamford in Lincolnshire to Banbury, whose symbol is a shell found in the rock of the Jurassic limestone ridge which the path follows. At the bottom of the slope, go through the kissing gate (*not* through the small wooden gate on the right), and turn right to walk with the brook and the fish ponds of Wardington Manor on the right. This path leads into the village of **Upper Wardington**. Bear right up onto the main village street by the Plough Inn.

Access Point: Upper Wardington, 4.5 miles. Telephone and pub. Limited car parking. GR 497460.

Turn left on Thorpe Road to walk south. Walk out of the village ignoring the first footpath sign to the right, but take the second footpath on the right just before the de-restriction sign. Bear diagonally left (SW 205°) to the gate in the field corner and follow the path on the left side of the hedge. Continue in the same direction (205°), then alongside three more fields, keeping the left side of the hedge. On reaching a field with prominent ridge and furrow keep on in the same direction to a gate and stile on the far side. We saw redwings in these fields in winter. Walk under the railway bridge built of engineering bricks, dark blue in colour. Keep straight ahead on the path and over the footbridge into Northamptonshire. Here the Oxfordshire/Northamptonshire county boundary follows this minor tributary of the River Cherwell. Walk south past the grassy irregularities which are the remains of the deserted medieval part of the village of **Chacombe**. Where the path meets Silver Street near a wooden bench, bear right to walk towards the Inn.

Deserted and shrunken settlements

These are common in parts of Middle England. The reasons for settlement shrinkage are complex and include soil exhaustion, climate deterioration, epidemic disease as a consequence of decades of malnutrition. Diversification of farming followed: sheep were raised in place of corn. People were forced off the marginal lands or were attracted to fill up spaces caused by disease in settlements that had more fertile land.

It is worth taking a short diversion here to see the church by turning sharp right into Church Lane. Keys are kept with either the churchwardens, Mrs Wintersgill, 2 Wesley Place, (Tel: 01295 712290), or Mr Bricknell, The Poplars, Oxford Road, (Tel: 01295 710050). The church porch is medieval with a wooden door and ironwork. The font is early Norman (12th century) and is associated with the baptism of St Rumbold in 622 AD. St Rumbold was a local saint and legend says that as soon as he was born, he demanded baptism, preached a sermon and died three days later. After he died, his holy relics were dug up every five years and buried for luck in the surrounding villages, but in the end no-one could remember in which village he was last buried.... Other church treasures include a medieval altar, one of the few survivors after the Reformation, with five consecration crosses (to represent the five wounds of Christ) carved into the roughly-hewn stone slab. At the dedication of the altar, holy oil would have been poured into the five crosses to consecrate it.

There is, likewise, a pre-Reformation brass and a medieval wall-painting depicting St Peter being crucified upside-down. On a pillar beside the font, is an old 'graffito' of a mitred bishop irreverently depicted as a bumble-bee!

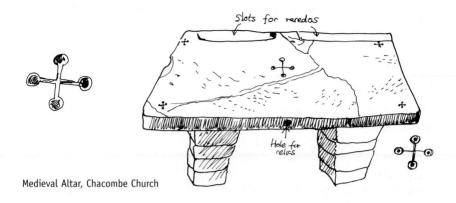

Medieval Altar, Chacombe Church

Access Point: Chacombe, 6 miles.
George and Dragon Inn. Telephone
and post office. GR 491438.

Church Lane leads back to the village
street to pass the George and Dragon PH,
a 17th century inn. Turn right into Silver
Street to pass the pub and, keeping to the
left of the small village green, turn left to
walk eastwards for a few paces along the
main village street. Turn right at the footpath sign along a gravel drive, through
an iron kissing gate, alongside a house,
then bear left away from the house to go
through another kissing gate, across a
stable yard and turn right onto a tarmac
driveway to Chacombe House (now a

Graffito at Chacombe Church

nursing home). At the gates of the park, turn left before the cattle grid and through
a kissing gate into a yew plantation. There are old yew trees here and a curious holly
with flat leaves. On leaving the wood, *do not* go over the stile to the left but go
straight ahead (SE 155°) beside a golf course, then across a fairway and over a footbridge towards the tall white-painted footpath posts on the same compass bearing.
The remains of the ridge and furrow ploughing are remarkable here. Aim for the
right of a tall clump of trees and go over a stile out of the golf course into the open
fields. Continue in the same direction uphill along a fieldpath on a bank. Where a
hedge starts, keep on the left side of it. At the point where a farm track crosses, bear
left (SE 142°), under a pylon towards **Middleton Cheney**. Cross the road with care

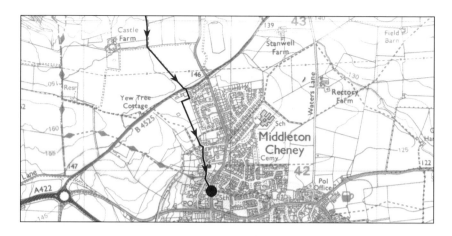

and continue on the path behind the houses towards the church spire. At the end of the field, turn right, then left into a narrow, fenced footpath. At the road, turn left and first right into the village street towards the church which has beautiful William Morris and Burne-Jones windows. The key is available either from the Rectory at 3, High Street (situated between the Dolphin and the Red Lion), (Tel: 01295 710254) or at Brazenose Cottage, 47, High Street, (Tel: 01295 711168). The key fits the small door in the north wall of the church, near the iron gate leading from Glovers Lane. NB. The key goes in upside down and turns the opposite way to normal!

For car parking, turn left at a small triangular green just after the church and bear right to reach the High Street, where there are public houses, a telephone and shops.

Day Five

MIDDLETON CHENEY TO SOULDERN

Middleton Cheney GR 500422 to Souldern GR 520315

The journey continues south, with the River Cherwell forming much of the boundary. The canal-side walk gives an insight into the transport of goods before the railway and the motorway. We pass the fifty miles point in Souldern where the day ends, as it began, with a chamfered corner.

Distance: 10 miles (16 km).

Maps: Explorer 206 – Edge Hill and Fenny Compton.
Explorer 191 – Banbury, Bicester and Chipping Norton.
Landranger 151 – Stratford-upon-Avon and surrounding area.

Transport: King's Sutton railway station (1.1 miles from route).
National Rail enquiries – Tel: 0845 7484950.

Taxis: Banbury • ABC Taxis – Tel: 01295 258888/268888.
• Banbury Taxis – Tel: 01295 263838/267878.
King's Sutton • Waverley Garage (Roger Moon) –
Tel: 01295 811274.

Car Parking: Middleton Cheney – High Street near Red Lion public house.
Souldern – in the main village street near to the entrance of Fox Lane.

Accommodation/Public Houses/Refreshments:
King's Sutton (1.4 miles from route)
• White Horse Inn PH – Tel: 01295 810843.
• Butchers Arms PH – Tel: 01295 810898.
• College Farmhouse (B&B), Astrop Lane –
Tel: 01295 811473.
Aynho Wharf • The Great Western Arms PH – Tel: 01869 338288.
• Wharf shop – snacks, open summer only.
Aynho (1.4 miles from route)
• Cartwright Arms Hotel – Tel: 01869 811111.
Souldern • Fox Inn, Fox Lane – Tel: 01869 345284.
• Tower Fields, B&B, Tusmore Road – Tel: 01869 346554.

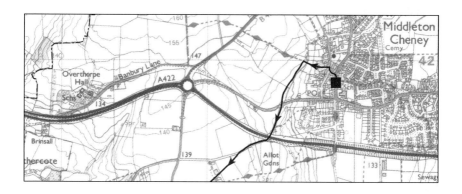

From the Red Lion pub in **Middleton Cheney**, walk north along the High Street, past the Baptist church, then bear left along an alley between houses to join Church Lane. Bear right past a small triangular green just south of Middleton Cheney church. Turn almost immediately left (W) onto a path between houses just before a shop called 'Parkinsons'.

The stone house on the left-side of this path has a chamfered corner. This was to enable carts, in the days of horse-drawn waggons, to turn without brushing against any sharp corner thus knocking off the load.

A chamfered corner, Middleton Cheney

Walk west down through the field, cross the bridge built of old railway sleepers and turn left, leaving the Jurassic Way. Walk along the right (W) side of the brook.

Cross the road and walk south along the minor road which has been truncated by the bypass. Pass through some wooden barriers to cross the bypass and rejoin the Warkworth road. Walk for 240 yards, then go through a field gate on the left, with a horses' stable in the right corner, and cross the stile opposite. Turn right through another metal gate into a jumping paddock and follow the right-hand fence to the hedge and wire fence. At the time of writing, there was no stile out of the field so climbing over the barbed wire is the only option. In the field beyond, bear left (W 228°) to the far hedge, aiming left of the large barn ahead. At present, there is no stile to exit the field, so turn left and follow the hedge to use the stile further south, which is on the Jurassic Way. Cross the stile into a paddock behind the buildings on the route of the Jurassic Way and bear left (SW) across the field to the gap in the hedge. Bear left (south) again to leave the Jurassic Way, through two fields to join the road to **Warkworth** (205°).

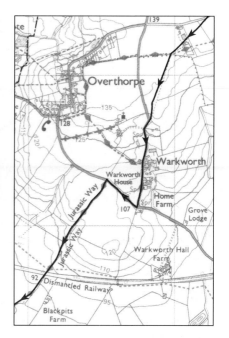

The church of Warkworth can be seen, isolated from the village. This has resulted from settlement shift since medieval times, presumably to be closer to the road and the spring.

Access point: Warkworth, 1.4 miles. Very limited car parking. GR 488404.

Walk past the fine buildings of Home Farm and Warkworth House and on to the road junction. Turn right at the road signed 'Overthorpe' and walk for 0.3 miles, then turn left along the Jurassic Way on a bridleway down towards the motorway. The traffic roar increases on approaching the M40. Continue downhill over the line of a dismantled railway. At a field gate just beyond the second pond, turn left at the footpath sign, and walk half-left up the slope to cross a wooden-planked and brick-built Victorian railway bridge. Go straight ahead along the right side of a field boundary. Turn left (S) alongside the motorway for 200 yards, then right under the

Oxford Canal swing-bridge, south of Banbury

motorway to walk beside the river Cherwell for 150 yards. The river forms the county boundary here. Turn left over a wooden footbridge dedicated to Dick Smith 'a rambler whose extraordinary efforts inspired the building of this bridge'. The deep brown colour of the river water is due to the leaching of the iron from the ironstone into the ground water. We saw iridescent, turquoise dragonflies here in June. Walk away from the river (216°) to the hedge corner and go along the right side of the hedge towards the Oxford Canal. On reaching the canal bridge, turn left where the path joins the Oxford Canal Walk. There are a series of swing-bridges, which allow farm vehicles to cross fields divided by the canal. It is a world apart from the busy motorway.

Continue south under the motorway, past Grant's Lock to Twyford Wharf. The map shows that the River Cherwell forms the county boundary. The spire of King's Sutton church is clearly visible ahead on the left. Pass Twyford Wharf and continue on under the bridge. Just past these bridges there are deserted buildings on the right bank, which were kilns for the brick-making industry. Bricks were often fired locally to the construction project, eliminating the need for further transport.

At the next curve in the canal, the county boundary and the route of the River Cherwell coincide as the ancient course of the river was originally along this part of

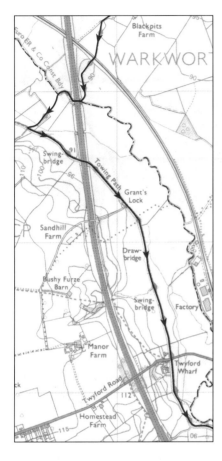

the canal. Otherwise, the county boundary is close to the canal along the current route of the River Cherwell, which is about 15 feet below us to our left, just visible through the blackthorn thicket. The canal route is on a raised embankment and there are sluice gates at regular intervals to drain off excess water.

A line of pollarded willow trees marks the twisting course of the river across the flood plain. This river valley is

Oxford Canal, sluice gate

used as a 'corridor' of communication – first the river, then the canal, the railway and, last of all – and the most intrusive, the motorway. The roads are, for the most part, situated higher up on the valley sides away from the risk of flooding. Some of the ancient ways are indicated by the delightful series of wrought-iron gates leading on from the swing bridges on the left. They have a grace and charm of their own.

A few yards further on, past support structures of an old railway bridge, there is a stone. This originally had a cast-iron plate indicating the distance to Banbury but it was removed in World War II to prevent German paratroopers finding their way.

Walk on and under the motorway again. The county boundary is now further away as it follows the course of a former meander in the River Cherwell but then runs beside the canal, so that we are walking along the Oxfordshire/Northamptonshire border. This part of the path was delightfully 'jungly' in June. There were yellow flag irises, meadowsweet and Himalayan balsam flowering when we walked by, and bulrushes in the winter.

Walk past the Old Wharf which would have originally handled the coal barges.

Oxford Canal and its Trade

The Oxford Canal was opened in 1778 before the development of the railways. It was significant as a carrier of bulk commodities such as coal from Coventry to Newbury; plaster from Barrow-upon-Soar to Thatcham; hides from Birmingham to Reading; slates from North Wales to London; and agricultural produce to the North. The canal was also an important source of income generated by the servicing of vessels as well as canal-side industries such as lime-burning and brick-making in kilns. There was a daily 'fly' boat service to London and to give an example of the intensity of the traffic in 1842, an average of 190 boats per week passed over Claydon summit lock (see day 3) carrying their merchandise. The local cost of coal dropped substantially due to canal transport.

(Source Trinder, B. *Victorian Banbury*, Phillimore 1982).

Former wharves, Twyford Lock

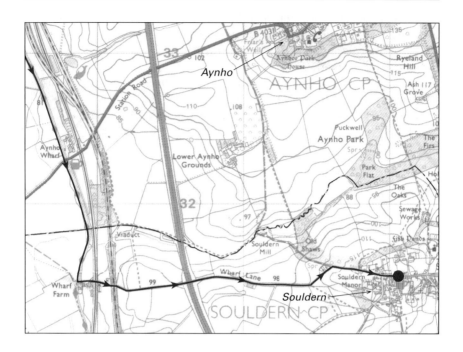

Pass another swing bridge, then at Nell Bridge Lock, cross the Aynho to Adderbury road with care and rejoin the right (W) side of the canal. 550 yards further on, the River Cherwell and with it the county boundary, cross the Oxford Canal. The river makes a sufficient cross current to make unwary barges hit the right bank. The raised causeways are built of dark engineering brick for the barge horses to use in former times. This causeway crosses the lively Cherwell River by means of a viaduct, so it is possible to sit actually on the middle of the county boundary with Northamptonshire to the east and Oxfordshire to the west!

Walk on down the towpath to Aynho Wharf on the east bank (shop and public house) and easy access to **Aynho** village (1.4 miles) with accommodation if needed. We saw grey wagtails and kingfishers along this stretch. Walk on south, past another milestone just before reaching Wharf Farm bridge. Again there are only four holes marking where the cast iron distance plate was bolted on. Wharf Farm bridge has elliptical arches made of brown brick, typical of the Banbury area, and has sandstone copings (shaped stones along the top of a bridge). This is quite different in design from that of the bridges nearer Oxford which have semi-circular arches. At this bridge, go through the wrought-iron gate and turn left (E) over the canal and into Wharf Lane heading away from the canal towards the village of **Souldern**. First cross over the Oxford–Banbury railway bridge, then under the bridge of the

Banbury–Bicester line. On approaching the motorway, there are good views of Aynho Park House with its adjoining church. The house (open May–Sept on Weds & Thurs, 2–5pm), has a planted parkland with wide vistas.

Go up the road, bearing right where the lane from Souldern Mill joins from the left, and continue into the village past the great gate pillars of Souldern Manor on the right where, at GR 519315, we are now fifty miles along the Seven Shires Way from Day 1 start point. At the corner of Fox Lane is another house with a chamfered corner, just as in Middleton Cheney at the start of the walk.

Day Six

Souldern to Finmere

Souldern GR 520315 to Finmere GR 636330

A day travelling eastwards to meet the fifth shire, Buckinghamshire. We pass through the tiny hamlet of Juniper Hill or 'Larkrise' of Flora Thompson fame and cross the infant River Great Ouse on its journey east to the Wash.

Distance: 11.2 miles (16.9 km).

Maps: Explorer 191 – Banbury, Bicester and Chipping Norton.
Explorer 192 – Buckingham and Milton Keynes.
Landranger 151 – Stratford-upon-Avon and surrounding area.
Landranger 152 – Northampton and Milton Keynes area.
Landranger 165 – Aylesbury and Leighton Buzzard area.

Taxis: Brackley   • P.J.Cars – Tel: 01280 704330.
Buckingham   • Buckingham Taxis – Tel: 01280 812038.
               • Kings of Buckingham – Tel: 01280 815519.

Car Parking: Souldern – in the main village street near to the entrance of Fox Lane.
Finmere – by the triangular green at the bottom of the slope below the church.

Accommodation/Public Houses/Refreshments:

Juniper Hill   • Southview B&B – Tel: 01869 810815.
Westbury   • Reindeer Inn PH – Tel: 01280 704934.
               • Mill Farm House B&B – Tel: 01280 704843.
Little Tingewick, near Finmere
               • Red Lion Inn B&B and others in Finmere –
                 Tel: 01280 848285.

Cherwell Valley Tourist Information Centre – Tel: 01869 345888 or Bicester TIC – Tel: 01869 369055 for full list of accommodation.

Locomotive-shaped topiary, Souldern

Continue along **Souldern** village street south-east from Fox Lane, past the loco-motive-shaped topiary of a high yew hedge on the right.

Pass the village pond and out of the village to reach the B4100. Turn right, then left onto a minor road signposted 'Tusmore', past Tower Fields. This is a long straight road formed after the 18th century Enclosure Acts. There were white violets and

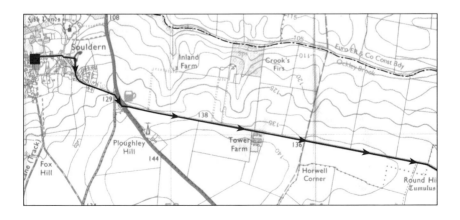

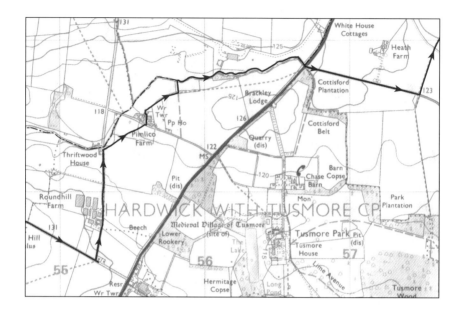

celandines on the banks when we walked there in March. The county boundary is two fields to the left (N) following the course of Ockley Brook. The two large round red balls visible are the radio station of RAF Croughton. Walk past Round Hill tumulus on the right side, then take the minor road to the left, sign-posted 'Croughton', past Roundhill Farm. At Thriftwood House take the path diag-onally right to the large grey steel gate. Go through the gate and aim for the centre of the farm buildings and the wooden gate just behind the electricity pylon in the field. Dog-leg right and left to the farmyard entrance and out through the double gates at rear. The ponds and Ockley Brook are visible. *Do not* follow the path to these ponds, but turn right along the left side of the hedgerow running parallel to the brook.

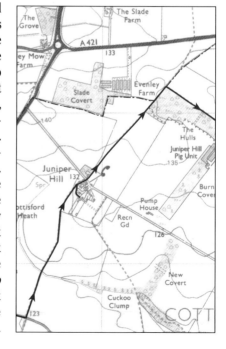

Go through the gap in the hedge of this first field, then turn left to follow the hedgerow by the bridleway to the double-gated bridge over Ockley Brook and into Northamptonshire. Turn right to keep close to the curving course of the brook and continue along it until you reach a gap in the barrier leading out onto the busy A43(T) dual carriageway. Cross it with great care, then go along the road to Cottisford. *Do not* take the bridleway on the right signed 'Hardwick'. Walk past Heath Farm, then after one field turn left (N) at a footpath sign to Juniper Hill. Walk on the right side of the hedge in the first field, then on the left of the hedge on the headland provided by the farmer. Continue left of the paddocks into a lane leading into the hamlet of **Juniper Hill**.

Access Point: Juniper Hill, 4.6 miles. Telephone. GR 578325.

Lark Rise to Candleford

Juniper Hill is the setting of Flora Thompson's autobiographical account of her childhood in '*Lark Rise to Candleford'*. The names of the people and places are based on reality. To make the 100 yard diversion to see Flora's childhood home, turn right into the lane at the back of the village by the paddocks. Pass a house on the left called 'The Old Meeting Place', then, on the right, are a pair of white gate posts leading to a tiny, white-painted cottage where Flora Thompson lived, just by the edge of Lark Rise field in the direction from which we have come. The wall plaque indicates 'Flora Thompson, authoress lived here 1876–1947'. It is private property so please just view from the lane. Just past the cottage on the right, is a much restored stone cottage called 'Queenies' in reference to the character Queenie in the novel.

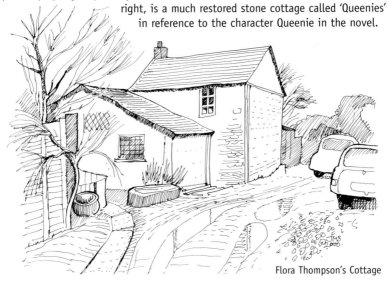

Flora Thompson's Cottage

To continue the walk, retrace your steps along the lane to rejoin the track leading to the road. Cross the road and continue along the grassy track, go over a stile and into a field. Here, in October, we saw a young hedgehog curled up in the defensive position. Continue along the right side of the hedge, and halfway along the field, bear half-right (045°) across the field to the left hand edge of the wood in front of you. Follow the edge and go through a gap in the hedge beside the ancient woodland bank surrounding the coppiced trees. This is the Northamptonshire/Oxfordshire county boundary which continues in the same direction as a ditch. At the corner of the wood, turn right through a small wooden gate, and go along the edge of the wood. On arriving at the road, turn left (NE). This is a good example of an enclosure road with wide verges and hedges which was used as a drove road.

Drove Roads

These were very wide, grassy roads used by drovers herding their livestock and geese from Wales and the West Country towards London. On arriving in fields near London the animals were fattened and taken to Smithfield Market. The owners of Monks House Farm, on the left of the road, told us that sheep are still driven along this road.

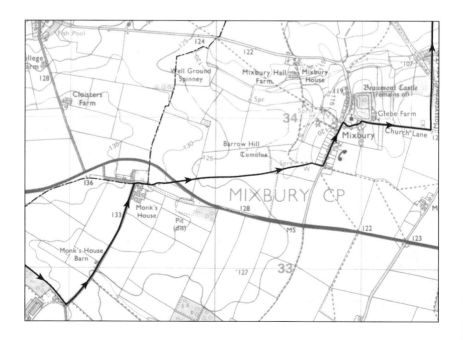

Pass the long farm buildings of Monks House Farm, originally a large monastic farming complex. Turn right onto the no-through road signposted 'Bridleway (private road)'. Go through the gate, and 50 yards ahead cross a ditch and a stile in the left-hand hedge. Bear right over the field to cross the main road by two stiles. Aim to the right of **Mixbury** village (080°). Go over a stile, a bridge and another stile, then across the next field towards the galvanised iron gate by two ash trees. Take the stile through the hedge into a small field left of the gate. Go through two horse paddocks via two stiles, across a track, to some poplar trees, where there is a double stile in the hedge. There are some humps and bumps in the land here. These are the remains of house platforms of a larger village (as at Chacombe in Day 4) that reduced in size due to the deaths caused by the plague. At the end of the third paddock pass through an iron gate along the track to emerge on the village street at a house called 'The Old Forge'. Turn left and walk towards Mixbury church.

There are some good examples of houses that have been built matching the original vernacular style. There are also some fine examples of cast iron garden railings which are relatively rare, as many were melted down to make steel during the Second World War.

Access Point: Mixbury church, 7.3 miles. GR 609340.

When you reach the church (key held at 2, Church View), bear right through the churchyard, past the original school room by the far gate, to turn right along the road. Ramparts can be seen through the hedge on the left. This is all that remains of Beaumont Castle, a motte and bailey castle built in the 12th century. Walk along Church Road to then turn left (N) onto a bridleway called Mossycorner Lane leading towards Westbury. Go under the bridge of the former Great Central Railway from Marylebone in London to the North Midlands. The bridge is also made of dark engineering bricks as at Chacombe (Day 4). Keep north along the

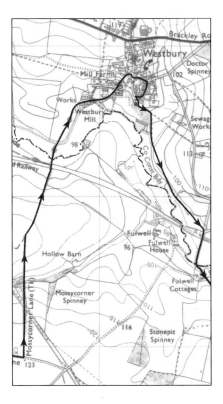

left side of the hedgerow on the bridleway down to the river and cross another dismantled railway. This originally led from Banbury to Bedford via Bletchley. Continue on the track to a river bridge. The river is the Great Ouse in its infancy whose source is north of Syresham, a village north-east of Brackley. The river winds its way from here through Bedfordshire and Cambridgeshire, turns north to empty into the North Sea at Kings Lynn on the Wash. It is a narrow river here but marks the county boundary. Wild brown trout weighing up to nearly 1kg enjoy its waters and we saw a grass snake on its bank in July. Cross it into **Buckinghamshire**, our fifth shire.

The three counties meet 0.75 miles west on the former railway line (GR 606356). The large field beyond the river is called 'Three Counties' reflecting the proximity of this meeting place. We looked for the boundary stone at the junction of the three counties, but found no sign of it. Continue walking away from the river following the left side of a former stone causeway across the water-meadow. There are signs of former water management and a mill leat.

Causeways
You will notice that there are numerous causeways across the fields bordering rivers. This is because in winter these fields used to flood. More efficient drainage and lower water tables mean that these causeways are no longer used.

Raised causeway, south of Westbury

Cross 'Three Counties' to the end of the track at the far side, and curve right towards some sheds to the right of the gate into the courtyard of a former mill. Walk through the courtyard and take the road up to the village of **Westbury** noting the high wall of the former manor house on the right. The use of different building materials is apparent – limestone and ironstone. Ignore all the footpath signs to right and left but continue to the small triangular green past Mill Farm House. Straight ahead (N) on the main street is a public house, the Reindeer.

Access Point: Westbury village green, 9.1 miles. Post office. GR 622357.

Turn right at the green along Fulwell Road and pass one of the lodge houses of the former manor house which is now Beachborough School. As the main street descends, turn right into Orchard Place, signposted to the church. On reaching the churchyard gates, take the footpath left through the churchyard. There are some remarkable terracotta urns used as gravestones here. Leave the churchyard and its ancient yew trees via a wooden hand-gate, continue through a garden to a new metal kissing gate. Cross a stile to go right downhill by the side of the wood. In January, the bank of the moat inside the wall was a mass of winter aconites. On arriving at the end of the boundary of the manor, walk to the end of the field where there is a small planked footbridge over a stream. Pieces of discarded railway line from the dismantled line two fields away have been used as some of the fence posts. Cross the bridge and keep in the same direction (163°) along the right hedge boundary by the brook. The path goes through the remains of a hedge, via a stile below an isolated barn. Keep to the left of the line of hawthorn trees (140°) from the path near the barn. As the path crosses the line of a former hedgerow, the twin arches of the disused railway can be seen. The path meets the road just left of Station House, a reminder of the former railway. Turn right and walk along the road. There is a modern causeway, similar to the one in the water-meadows south-west of Westbury. Black engineering bricks have been used and concrete slabs cover a former stone causeway. Re-cross the Great Ouse river back into Oxfordshire. The cottages up the hill on the right are called Fulwell Cottages, a reference to the former fulling mills.

Fulling Mills

In medieval times the Great Ouse had a sufficiently forceful water flow to power fulling mills along its banks. These mills were part of the earliest industrial revolution in the 12th and 13th centuries. The water-driven hammers pounded the woollen cloth, and with Fuller's Earth, a kind of clay which removed the natural grease, the cloth felted and therefore became denser and warmer to wear. Before this development a particularly unpleasant task was that of the 'walkers', the men who trod down the cloth in large troughs of cold water. Hence the relatively common surname of 'Walker'.

We heard and saw a variety of birds as we walked on this road; great spotted woodpeckers in the wood on the left, and lapwing, fieldfare, common or grey partridge and yellowhammers in the fields and hedges to the right. Walk up the road with fine views of the Great Ouse valley to your left, past Tile House Farm, then two fields later and 550 yards past the hedge boundary to the left, there is a footpath sign. Go through the kissing gate left from the road. Keep to the right of the old hedgerow, over the wooden stile, and walk diagonally left across the field towards the right of a paddock and aim slightly right of **Finmere** church. Cross a stile, turn left along a grassy track and over two stiles into a football pitch. Follow the path round to the right, past a play area and out onto the road through a wooden gate near the church, turn right down the slope to the triangular green.

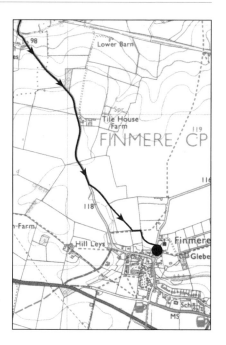

Day Seven

FINMERE TO LUDGERSHALL

Finmere GR 636330 to Ludgershall GR 660172

This day marks the gradual change of the landscape as we walk through Oxfordshire and Buckinghamshire. The Aylesbury clay vale provides no stone, so many houses are built of brick. Much of the land has been reclaimed from marsh; village names give clues to the watery surroundings.

Distance: 10.2 miles (16.3 km).

Maps: Explorer 192 – Buckingham and Milton Keynes.
Explorer 180 – Oxford, Witney and Woodstock.
Landranger 165 – Aylesbury and Leighton Buzzard area.

Taxis: Bicester   • Bicester Taxis – Tel: 01869 242424/252525/323232.
• ABC Taxis – Tel: 01869 242601/242526.

Car Parking: Finmere – by the triangular green at the bottom of the slope below the church.
Ludgershall – limited parking by the church or on road north of church.

Accommodation/Public Houses/Refreshments:
Poundon   • Sow and Pigs PH – Tel: 01869 277728.
• Manor Farm B&B – Tel: 01869 277212.
Marsh Gibbon   • The Greyhound Inn – Tel: 01869 277365.
• The Plough PH – Tel: 01869 278759/277305.
• Judges Close B&B – Tel: 01869 278508.
Ludgershall   • Bull and Butcher PH – Tel: 01844 238094.
• The Briars B&B – Tel: 01844 237721.
• Poletrees Farm B&B – Tel: 01844 238276.
  (0.75 miles south from route).

Finmere's place name reflects the marshy environment, *mere* being the Old English for lake. From the lane south of the church, continue to walk due south through the village along Valley Road and cross the now closed section of the B4031. Go down the farm track ahead, across the new bypass with care to Gravel Farm, through three steel gates and across two fields. In the third field, the path follows about 50 yards parallel to the hedge (225°). Go under the National Grid line, keep left of the pond. At the far end of the field, beyond the kink in the hedgerow, turn left (E) through a steel field gate onto the bridle track to cross the busy A421, also the county boundary, into Buckinghamshire. The field ahead was previously a Second World War airfield, but now is used for private flying and a Sunday market. Take the bridleway bearing right (SE 176°) to a group of trees on the far side of the field sheltering a house with a tall brick chimney, *not* towards the farm building with the pale corrugated-iron roof visible from the road. On nearing the house, go through the small wooden gate left of the group of trees, then along the farm track. There is ridge and furrow on both sides. At the lane, turn left, then right before Manor Farm in the hamlet of **Barton Hartshorn**. The farm has a fine stone archwayed entrance. Walk along the lane to just before a corrugated-iron shed on the right side, then turn half-left keeping left of two solitary trees in the field (125°). Walk up to the line of telegraph posts. If you look back in winter when the trees are bare, you will see Barton Harsthorn Tudor manor

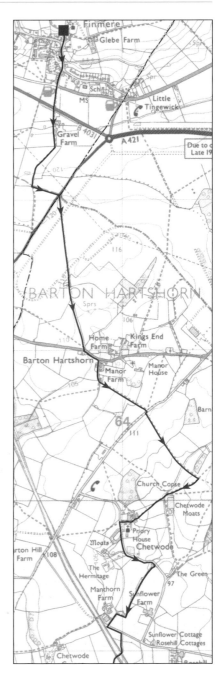

house. A fingerpost at a field gate indicates the way to cross the lane, through two fields, and over a brook in a south-easterly direction. Walk just past the fir plantation on the left, then turn sharp right (SW) to Chetwode Moats (fishponds) and a copse at the bottom of the slope. We found in the light soils, Neolithic flint scrapers that were used to trim bone, wood or hides. Go through the corner of the wood across a foot-bridge, to cross a second footbridge and stile, then half-left up the left side of a line of ancient trees aiming for some trees left of farm buildings. Go to the corner of a wooden-railed fence, turn half-right at the fence corner through a gate and farmyard to the road and turn left. There is a splendid avenue of lime trees with Chetwode Priory to the left.

Chetwode parish church is all that remains of a medieval priory founded by the Augustinian canons in 1245. The five 13th century lancet windows are remarkable, as are the stone sedilia (seats for the priests) and the detail of the stone carving. The lozenge-shaped, painted, wooden boards hanging on the walls are funeral hatchments or coverings, which bear the coat of arms of the family and were placed on the coffin.

Access Point: Chetwode Priory, 2.6 miles. GR 640298.

Continue on the road past Priory House. If you look right, through a gateway just beyond the Priory, the remains of the original moat are visible. Continue on down the winding lane, and 500 yards on, almost hidden in the trees on the right side of the road, is a decorated horse watering trough (1869) with the inscription 'Praise God from whom all Blessings flow'. Turn right 10 yards past the water well and follow the hedge on the right (SW) along the L-shaped field, until you are level with with Sunflower Farm. Continue walking along the footpath around the right-hand corner of the field to the left-hand side of the buildings at Manthorn Farm. Turn left along the lane for 100 yards, then right through a wooden kissing gate on the right side of some double steel gates.

Follow the gravel track and cross the dismantled Great Central railway, then bear left along the gravel track, dog-leg right and left on a long straight track towards **Godington**. We saw a grass snake here in June on the fine and sandy soil. On reaching a plantation of cypress trees, the track divides, go slightly left along the edge, then over the brook, which is the county boundary, from Buckinghamshire into Oxfordshire. Walk straight up, over a new bridge and out onto the road into the hamlet of Godington.

On reaching the lane, turn right for 180 yards, do not take the track through the farm on the left, but walk further along the lane (SW), noting how wide it is.

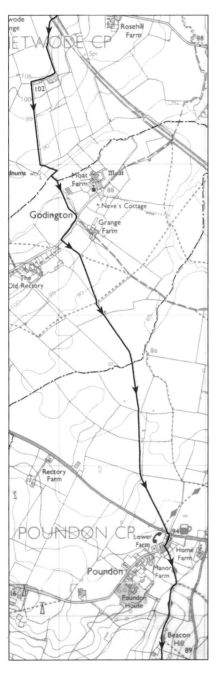

Moat Farm

There is an optional diversion of 0.5 miles (including return) to see both the church and Moat Farm. If you would like to do this, turn left at the road and walk north-east. The farmhouse dates from the 17th century and has a typical medieval moat. Moats were dug more for a status symbol than for defensive purposes and many did not encircle the house. Retrace your steps to Grange Farm.

It was another former drove road. Halfway along the field past Grange Farm and before the row of houses, turn left over a footbridge and a double stile. Cross the field to a stile on the far side. The path branches right (166°). Aim for a derelict, flat-topped corrugated-iron roofed barn in the corner of the next field. A wooden footbridge crosses to a track beside the one tree along the hedgerow. Turn left, and at the barn, continue by bearing further right (E 150°) to cross the field to a steel handrailed bridge on the Oxfordshire/Buckinghamshire county boundary.

Cross the next narrow field towards the plantation to another steel-railed footbridge crossing the ditch. Here, bear slightly more right (S 174°) through a plantation. The footpath is not marked, the ruts are deep, and it may be preferable to walk around the wood to the right, although this is not a right of way. At the other side, head for a stile in the corner of the field. Go along the left side of the next field, and over a stile where there is a pond with old willow trees. This originally provided a water source for the cattle in the four fields that merge at the pond. Continue on the right side of the hedge to a stile in the corner and continue towards the village of **Poundon** along part of the next field, then almost immediately left over the stile in the wire fence, then diagonally south-east (155°) to the corner. Cross two more fields and out onto the road over the stile, just right of the waterworks in the corner of the last field before the village. We saw field pansies when we walked through in May.

Access Point: Poundon, 5.7 miles. Telephone, pub. GR 647255.

Turn left to the public house. Here the footpath has been diverted. Take the road east, signposted 'Twyford and Marsh Gibbon', past the pub to the end of its garden. The footpath is now part of the Cross Bucks Way. Turn right (S) to walk in line with the houses, go over the next stile, then diagonally half-left away from the houses, over the stile, then turn right (S) to the stile in the corner of the next field. Cross uphill through the middle of the field to a stile just right of a wooden five-barred gate. The back of Poundon House is visible to the right with its fine, brick-walled kitchen garden and enormous greenhouses. Continue with the hedge on the left, past a pond towards a low building ahead. About halfway between the pond and the building is a stile to the left of a wooden gate, go over this and aim for **Marsh Gibbon** church tower to the south (180°). There are extensive views to the left across the

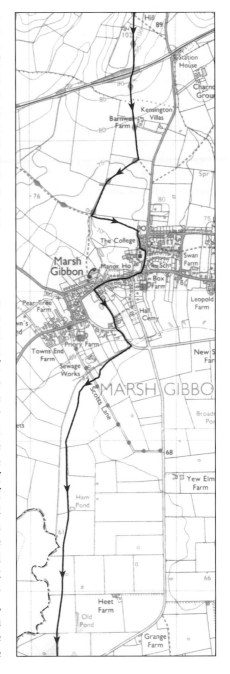

Vale of Aylesbury with a pattern of small fields and hedgerows. The stile out of this pasture is over the brow of the hill. Walk downhill nearly due south (185°). In the scrubland bordering the Bicester – Bletchley railway line, about halfway between the two downhill field hedges, is a scissor stile. Cross this and the railway with care, bear left on the footpath, even though the way indicated on the Explorer map bears right (W) immediately after the railway. The mound is the result of the upcast of the Victorian railway workings. Continue south along the left (E) side of the hawthorn copse. From here cross the field to the right of a farm and buildings called Kensington Villas. Bear slightly left to a stile/footbridge on the right side of a gate in the hedge. In the next field, bear diagonally half-right towards a Dutch barn, to a stile in the very corner. There are old clay quarry workings in this field. Continue straight ahead (S) on the left side of the hedgerow to a stile in the corner. Turn left here, bearing away from the right side of the hedge to pass on the right side of a ruined well-house. This would have formerly controlled the flow of water to the village. Walk across the ridge and furrow towards the far side of a tall white house, pass left of this and take the path right (S) via the stile. Take the right-hand lane that leads to Marsh Gibbon church. The houses are very low, the local building material being brick in contrast to the limestone of the northerly part of the boundary walk. There are several thatched houses, one of them is dated 1535. On arriving at the brick house called Sunnymead, take the alley-way left along the

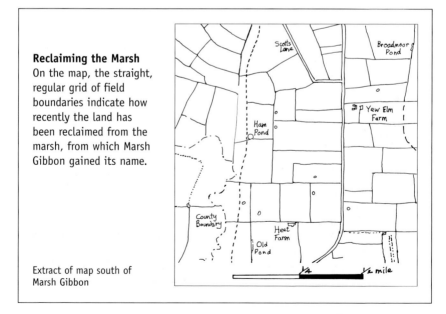

Reclaiming the Marsh
On the map, the straight, regular grid of field boundaries indicate how recently the land has been reclaimed from the marsh, from which Marsh Gibbon gained its name.

Extract of map south of Marsh Gibbon

churchyard wall. There is a fine Manor House beyond the church. On joining the road, turn right and cross over to the left-hand pavement for safety's sake as there is a dangerous bend.

Access Point: Marsh Gibbon church, 7.5 miles. Telephone, post office, shop, pubs. GR 648232.

Turn right at the Plough Inn and take the raised footpath on the right side of the village street. If you wish to make a diversion to the Greyhound Inn with its Thai cuisine, bear right at the village pond, if not, bear left and just beyond the pond, turn left (S) along Moat Lane. Walk past a thatched cottage past the public footpath sign and left past Grove House. Join Whales Lane out of the village, continue south, then just after steel railings on the right side and before a sharp road bend to the left, turn right (W) along the footpath on the left side of a hedge. Bear slightly left (SW) to the corner of the hedge and then through a kissing gate into Scotts Lane. Cross the lane and on through another kissing gate. Walk parallel to the long straight hedge (205°) towards the small field barn in the corner. Note the remains of ridge and furrow ploughing in the flat land.

On reaching the small brick field barn, go through the gate and walk on the west side of the hedgerow on the left-hand side of this L-shaped field. At the corner of this hedge, keep on in the same direction (180°) to the gate on the right of two willow trees.

Snipe

At this gate, there is a pond, Ham Pond, created to provide a water source to both fields. The place name Ham in Old English means homestead or *hamm* meaning meadow. The field beyond is large and flat with unobstructed views. It was a place well-known to one of our group, who taught glider pilots to make field landings here. The field is still being used for the same purpose. We startled a snipe here. These wading birds favour a wet habitat and the damp meadows are ideal for them to find the worms and surface living insects that form the bulk of their diet.

Cross the next field to a double gate. The hedge to the right of the footpath has an unusually winding nature. It marks the course of the River Ray, a tributary of the River Cherwell and forms the county boundary, Oxfordshire being on the far side and Buckinghamshire on the near side. Here we saw a flock of fieldfares heading south to their wintering quarters in Cornwall in late October. Go straight across the next field (S) to the double stile and footbridge in the hedge, to follow the hedge on the left through three more fields and onto the road. Turn right towards Piddington. Opposite is the sign of a permissive footpath that follows parallel on the south side of this small road, then returns onto it. This is an English Nature site of meadows of the Upper Ray river. These flood plains attract many species of waterfowl and wading birds in winter,

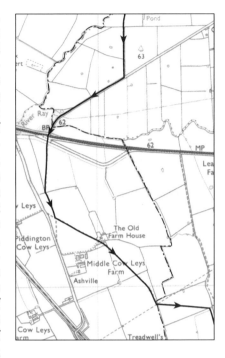

and unusual plant species grow here, including the cerise-coloured ragged robin. On nearing Akeman Street (now the A41), a former Roman road, cross the bridge of the River Ray. A cast-iron boundary post indicates entry back into Oxfordshire.

Boundary Post, River Ray

Cross Akeman Street (now the A41), which formerly connected St Albans (Verulamium) with Cirencester (Corinium) and which we cross again on Day19. Then make a small dog-leg, right (W) then left, through one set of steel gates, and travel east for a few yards along an asphalted lane. At the next steel gate, turn right (185°) over a ditch via a wooden footbridge. In May, the ditch had bulrushes, water mint and teasel growing in it. Cross the field to the far right corner and go over a stile by an oak tree. Then walk along parallel to the lane on the right (165°) to where the barbed-wire fence crosses. Bear half-left to The Old Farm House at the corner of the field. On reaching there, climb over the wire fence just in front of the house to cross the drive, and over a culvert into an orchard. Bear left (SE, 136°) and through the end hedge and across the field south eastwards. At present, the marked footpath should exit the field in the middle of the hedge but there is no gap or bridge, therefore, go to the right corner of the field where there is a gap (162°), then follow the track back left (E) along the south side of this hedge and halfway along to resume the right of way. Aim for the south-east corner of the field where the National Grid electricity lines cross the hedge. Just right (S) of one of the 'notches' or corners in the hedge, there is a deep ditch and stile. This is the Oxfordshire/Buckinghamshire county boundary. The 'stepped' effect of the interlocking of the former furlong blocks in determining the county boundary can be seen on the map immediately to the north (see also Day 4). Go diagonally right (SE) in the next field, to some willow trees in

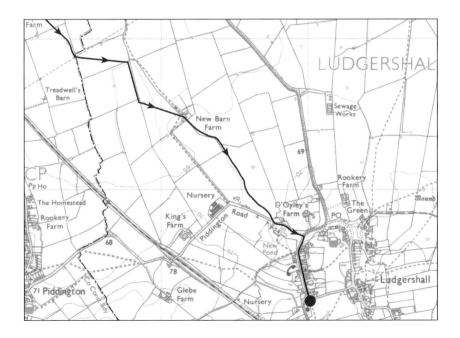

the far corner. This field shows the evidence of medieval ridge and furrow ploughing. Go over the stile and footbridge in the corner to follow the right side of the hedgerow south to the next field corner where there is another stile and footbridge across the ditch. Cross the next field diagonally left (SE) across a mid-field ditch to New Barn Farm. On the left side of the field, 25 yards before the corner, cross a stile and sleeper bridge, turn right between the ditch and the wooden fence to a small gate. Cross the farm access road and continue along the footpath left of the ditch. Follow this path for two fields on the left side of the hedgerow. The pronounced reverse 'S' bends of the ridge and furrow of the medieval ploughing are visible. In the second field, aim for the low, white, thatched cottage by the roadside in the corner of the field. Climb over the stile, turn left along the road to the village pond of **Ludgershall**. There are bulrushes here. Walk diagonally right (SE) across the village green. Join the wide village street going south by bearing right.

Ludgershall village street

The church of Ludgershall is well worth a visit. There is a Norman font dating from 1120, stone capitals with carvings of 14th century men in hoods and women in wimples, all interlocking arms, and a splendid hammerbeam roof with angels.

Stone capitals, Ludgershall church

Cob Walls

There are several low thatched cottages left of the churchyard entrance. Some of the walls of the buildings are made of cob, a mixture of mud, chopped straw and dung. Only in the parts of Oxfordshire where stone and brick were scarce in the 15th century will this building method be seen. There are only a few examples remaining — the end wall of Pear Tree Cottage Farm is one.

Day Eight

LUDGERSHALL TO WATERPERRY

Ludgershall GR 660172 to Waterperry GR 628064

We follow the boundary over Oxfordshire's Muswell Hill, then, despite the intrusion of the motorway, find an opportunity to visit a rare duck decoy and to enjoy the flowers of an ancient woodland in Hell Coppice. The day ends with a chance to visit the Waterperry Gardens.

Distance: 12.5 miles (20 km).

Maps: Explorer 180 – Oxford, Witney and Woodstock.
Landranger 164 – Oxford and surrounding area.

Taxis: Thame • Dencars – Tel: 01844 873105. Mobile: 07774 740080.
• Thame Taxis – Tel: 01844 215000/216161.

Car Parking: Ludgershall – limited parking by the church, or on road north of church.
Waterperry – in the Horticultural Centre overflow car park (right, just inside the garden entrance).

Accommodation/Public Houses/Refreshments:
Boarstall • Tower Farm B&B – Tel: 01844 237564.
• Village Farm House B&B – Tel: 01844 237433.
Horton-cum-Studley
• Otmoor Lodge Hotel and the Black Olive Restaurant –
Tel: 01865 351235. (Telephone in advance to order lunches).
• Studley Priory Hotel (bar lunches available) –
Tel: 01865 351203/351254.
Waterperry Common
• Common Leys Farm B&B, Waterperry Common –
Tel: 01865 351266. Mobile: 0802960651.
• Oaktree Copse B&B, Wood Farm, near Oxford –
Tel: 01865 351695. Mobile: 07715926850.
Waterperry • Holbeach B&B, Worminghall Road – Tel: 01844 339623.

Waterperry Horticultural Centre Tea Rooms 10am–4pm (lunches noon–2pm) –
Tel: 01844 338087.

Thame Tourist Office for comprehensive list of accommodation – Tel: 01844 212834.

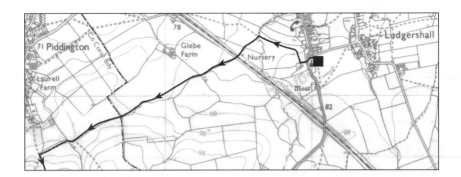

On leaving **Ludgershall** churchyard, turn right towards the village centre (N), then almost immediately left (W) across the road to a signed footpath over a stile and into an oblong field. Walk in a westerly direction to the right-hand end of the far hedge where there is a stile and bridge over the brook. We saw many butterflies in this clover-rich meadow including ringlet, meadow brown and gate keepers, when we walked through in late June. Turn left after the brook (235°) across the next field on the right side of the ditch, to the stile in the hedge. Part of the stile is made of a Great Western Railway broad gauge rail and dated 1908. We heard our first cuckoo of spring here on 28th April. Carry on along this path across the Marylebone/Princes Risborough to Bicester/Birmingham railway. This line will have strategic importance as part of the Channel Tunnel Link. There were cowslips out along this path and sky-larks singing. Continue walking west beyond the railway along the north side of the hedge. In winter the remains of the headlands are just visible: mounds of soil, now grassy, scraped off from the medieval ploughs as they were lifted at the end of each furrow. Go over another stile into the next field; the ridges and furrows are much closer together, there is no headland, and the ridge and furrow finishes before the hedge. This could be a much later feature, perhaps Victorian. The next hedge with the double stile and footbridge is the county boundary. Crossing into Oxfordshire, continue parallel along the right-hand side of the hedge (246°) through a long field (*not* through the first gate on the left or the first footpath sign on the left). Instead, use a footbridge (right of a water trough) to go over a brook, then turn right to follow the right-hand perimeter of the field. In winter this field is a remarkable example of ridge and furrow with very pronounced reverse 'S' bends. To the right are the buildings on the edge of the village of **Piddington**. On reaching the wide steel gate with the stile to the right, do not cross through, but instead turn sharply left (162°) and climb the slope, now walking in a south-easterly direction. Aim well to the left of the summit of Muswell Hill above, *not* along the hedge but towards the left of three willow trees in the top hedge of this field. As you reach the brow of the hill, a waymark becomes visible. A double stile and marked footbridge crosses to the next field. Follow the hedge on your left up towards Muswell Hill. This is part of the Piddington circular walk. Continue up the next two small fields and over the stiles. On the left is an ancient hedge and ditch. The group of ash trees at the summit is called the Wilderness. Ignore the first footpath sign to the left and continue up beside the trees to a gate which leads out onto an asphalted lane. This is the county boundary with Oxfordshire to the north and Buckinghamshire to the south. The fact that the county boundary is sited here is probably because, in the 10th and 11th centuries, the summit of Muswell Hill would have been a clear landmark for boundary making. There are extensive views to the north.

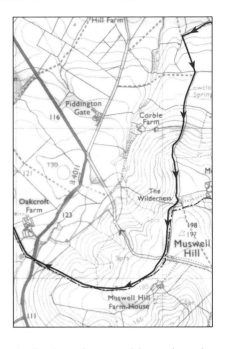

Walk along the lane beside the county boundary until a road is crossed. Turn right then left, enter the field opposite by the five-barred gate and keep along the right side of the left-hand hedge ahead, curving downhill south-west, then west, with Oakcroft Farm visible in the bottom of the valley. This old hedge is the county boundary. Continue down the hill, past some ancient oak trees to the road by a small gate. Turn right, then cross the road with care, noting the change in tarmac halfway between two gates (a modern indicator of the county boundary). Turn left through the five-barred gate to a footbridge and onto a bridle-track and up the hill to the left of Oakcroft Farm. Here, the boundary contains some ancient oak trees and several other stumps of old elm or oak. Follow the right side of the hedge. Notice how much it curves, a likely indicator of its antiquity. Continue on the bridleway which is still the boundary, until Little Wood is reached. Here, the path leaves the county boundary. Go half-left through the metal gate, then aim downhill towards the pylon on the land below to walk downhill on the right side of the hedge, ignoring the other metal gate close by on the left. Descend the hill for 50 yards, then at the hedge corner, turn left to follow the downhill side of the hedge along the contours of the hill. The Arncott munitions depot can be seen below and the noise of the M40 motorway traffic can be heard. This path to Oldhouse Spinney can be very boggy where springs ooze out. Go through the metal gate, turn uphill to walk along the right side of the hedge above. Twenty yards before a wooden stile at the end of this field, is a metal gate, turn left here.

N.B. It is possible to miss out Boarstall by following the path ahead across the golf-course on the footpath to the motorway bridge.

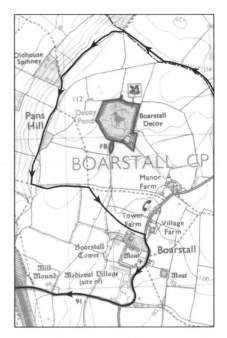

Walk south-east aiming right of the thick wood of Boarstall Nature Reserve (122°) to a stile in the next hedge. Then bear further right (S 165°) to the most southerly (right) of the two large trees. The path is not clear but at the next field boundary there is a kink in the hedge and a metal gate. Cross over the wooden stile left of the gate to continue walking (SE 178°), aiming left of the solitary tree in the field, to go through another metal barred gate.

Here there is another option. Should you wish to visit the Boarstall Decoy Nature Reserve, turn left (E) along the right side of the hedge through two fields to emerge on the Boarstall village road, just south of Manor Farm. Access to the Boarstall Decoy is via the track leading north-west just beyond the farm.

Boarstall Duck Decoy

This is one of only four decoys in working order in England. It appears on the maps of 1697. The decoy consists of a large pond with four 'pipes', covered with netting, into which the ducks were lured by food and the movement of a dog. Ducks have curious natures and move closer down the tunnel to watch the dog, which often wore a brightly coloured coat to attract their attention. The decoy was situated here, being close to the flooded Otmoor, a good habitat for ducks. As many as 800 were caught annually and records indicate that duck was regularly supplied for his Lordship's table at Boarstall Tower.

Now owned by the National Trust but incorporates a BBOWT (Berkshire, Buckinghamshire and Oxfordshire Wildlife Trust) nature reserve of 13 acres of woodland. Open 10–5 Wed, Sat, Sun & BHs. Tel: 01844 237488. Cost: £2.00, groups £1.00. Allow one hour for a visit.

Boarstall Duck Decoy

If you wish to miss out the Duck Decoy, bear half-left (SE 140°) from the second metal gate towards Tower Farm. Aim for the furthest right of three large hedgerow trees. Cross a footbridge between the second and third large trees, and in the next field, aim left of the farm buildings (133°), over a footbridge, through two metal gates, then bear right along the north side of Boarstall Tower and Tower Farm to the stile onto the road.

Boarstall Tower
The tall stone gatehouse is all that remains of a 14th century fortified house, long since demolished. It retains its crossloops for bows and is almost surrounded by a moat. (National Trust owned, open Wed & BH Mons 2–6, also Sat, by prior arrangement with tenant, write to Boarstall Tower HP18 9OX).

Turn right (S) past Boarstall Tower and the church, which is a Gothic rebuild after much damage in the Civil War. It has Jacobean carving. To the left (E), the village of Brill up on the hill can be seen. In the field to the right lumps and bumps can be seen in the grass - the remains of a medieval village shown on a rare map of 1444.

The village was perhaps larger than it is now or the settlement has shifted position. Walk along the road with great care, on the outside of the bends where necessary, for 0.25 miles, then straight ahead at the road junction in the direction of Murcott and Horton-cum-Studley. As the motorway is approached, in a field just beyond the brick built Cox's Cottage and stables, is a mill mound with a tree on the top of it. This is all that remains of a 17th century timber windmill.

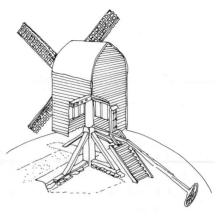

Take the road over the motorway and straight ahead. Just after a drive entrance from the left and where the

Reconstruction of a post mill, west of Boarstall

footpath joins the road at New Arngrove Farm, is the county boundary hedge. There was, until recently, a metal boundary post on the roadside verge, but now, again, it is the different quality of tarmac of Oxfordshire ahead and Buckinghamshire behind us that indicates the boundary. Walk for a further 0.3 miles, past Oakgrove Farm, before turning right along the drive to Warren Farm. Just before the farm, turn left

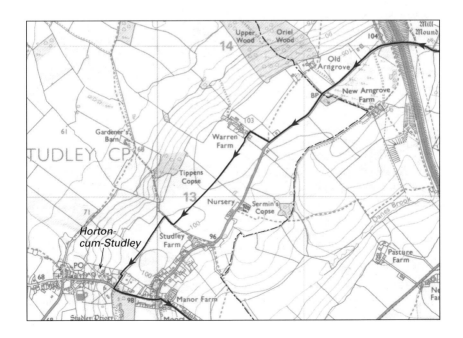

through the car park and along a marked footpath following the left side of the hedge. On reaching the end of this first field, continue on in the same direction with the power lines on your right side, to a gap in the hedge. The path crosses a gravelled road; turn right then almost immediately left across the field following the power lines, then along the path between houses in trees to reach the village street of **Horton-cum-Studley**, opposite the entrance to Studley Priory Hotel. Turn left uphill. To take a short diversion to the Black Olive Restaurant and other amenities, turn right downhill.

Access Point: Horton-cum-Studley, opposite Otmoor Lodge Hotel and Black Olive restaurant, 7.4 miles. Post office, village stores, telephone. GR 595125.

On retracing your steps up the village street right (E), a fine series of four brick almshouses are on the left side of the street. They were built in 1639, each with a double chimney and they retain their original doors. They are a good example of 17th century retirement homes.

At the road junction, turn right into Oakley Road (SE) towards Stanton St John and Brill. A flying pig, made of straw, is on the thatched ridge of the corner cottage. Continue along the road past Manor Farm, past the two footpaths

Horton-cum-Studley Church
The church just beyond the hotel by the crossroads was designed in 1867 by William Butterfield, the same Victorian architect who built Keble College in Oxford. The church is built with similar polychrome brickwork and is remarkably colourful inside.

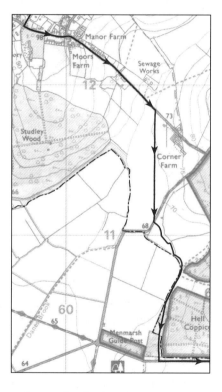

that enter from the left. Take the first footpath sign that leads right (S). Go into a paddock to a stile in the left hand corner, then due south (182°), walking through an oblong field aiming left of a group of large trees. Emerge from this field at a rusty metal gate just left (E) of the distinct turn in the road. Cross this minor road, which is the county boundary, into Buckinghamshire, and through a metal gate into a BBOWT Nature Reserve.

Alms Houses, Horton-cum-Studley

BBOWT owns about 90 precious nature reserves throughout this region and organises meetings, conservation working parties and educational programmes. BBOWT — Tel: 01865 775476.

Bear half-right (SE) towards and along the hedgerow on the left and left through a gap to turn right and follow closely the perimeter of an ancient hay meadow, rich with butterflies and flowers, including orchids. In the hedge corner, cross over the stile and footbridge to go through a thick hedgerow. Once out into the open, keep straight ahead along the left side of the hedge. This fine old hedge is the county boundary and to the east is a clearing in the wood with a high wooden hide on the woodland edge. Continue along the hedge then bear right at the corner of the clearing and into the wood to a waymark and follow the left side of the brook in what is called 'Hell Coppice'. The path can be unclear so follow the woodland bank (S 196°). This is ancient woodland and was part of the Bernwood Forest. It has many of the typical species: wood anemones, wild garlic or ramsons, primroses, ground ivy, celandine and violets, in a glorious spring patchwork of white, yellow and blues. For a 'whiff' of strong garlic, just touching the broad green leaves of the wild garlic is sufficient. This plant has white, star-like flowers that almost seem to glow in the deep woodland shade from April to June. The woodland boundary bank on the left is the county boundary but the existing woodland has encroached into the former field edge. Leave the wood by a stile to walk in the same direction (S) through a field, along the right side of Hell Coppice. Common hawthorn and the much less common woodland or midland hawthorn border this field and the dampness of the ground encourages the delicate pink flowers of lady's smock (or cuckoo flower) to flourish. Cross the stile at the end into a narrow path to the road. Turn left (E) along the road. The county boundary follows parallel to the road, just inside the wood on the left side of the road. At a slight 'S' bend in the road the tarmac line is evident, where the county boundary crosses to follow the south side.

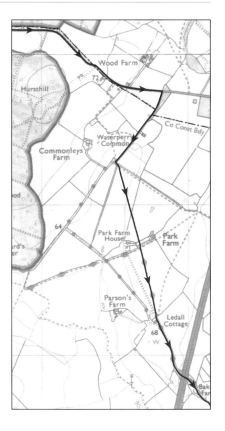

The boundary is an ancient hedge rich in woodland species. We listed oak, hazel, hawthorn, wild privet, field maple, briar rose, guelder rose, blackthorn and elm in this section, suggesting it is 800–900 years old.

0.75 miles along the road having passed a bed and breakfast opportunity (Oaktree Copse) on the right and Wood Farm on the left, turn right into Smiths Lane, a minor road leading south-west. This is a wide drove road, and passes a farm with a timber granary store with a tiled roof, now standing on breeze blocks, but would have originally stood on staddle stones.

At the bend in the tarmac road 250 yards past the farm, there is a copse with a footpath entering from the right. Turn left here, past the farm machinery, and walk for 20 yards to the corner of a large field with a Dutch barn and Park Farm House on the on the far side. Bear right across this field (172°), aiming for a large tree just left of the gabled and tiled roofs of the farm. Climb up the gentle hill, over the stile and footbridge, and along the left side of the farm garden. Should this stile be broken, turn left along the edge of the orchard, then right by the Dutch barn and back to the farm. The footpath goes across the field (SE 172°) to the brick-built Ledall Cottage (now Davenport House) at the far side of the field. If the path is obstructed by crops,

Farm granary

Staddle stones were originally used to improve ventilation and keep the rats out. The grain stores were always placed near to the farmhouse to protect a valuable resource, like having the bank under the farmer's eye!

turn right to walk to the farm entrance, then left along the track to the house. This is now part of the Oxfordshire Way, a long distance path from Bourton-on-the-Water to Henley-on-Thames. From Davenport House, walk along the lane (SE) across the bridge over the motorway and to the edge of **Waterperry** village. Take great care at the crossroads and continue along the wide street which is called Green Ground.

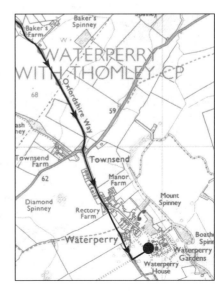

The word 'Ground' refers to the large-scale enclosures made for sheep farming in the open fields in the late Middle Ages. As the population declined after the Black Death, farmers switched to less labour-intensive sheep farming, another example of farmers needing to diversify.

Leave the road where it turns left at Manor Farm, and continue straight ahead through a wooden gate into a meadow. At the end of this field, a blue bridleway sign indicates the way forward to the south-east. On the left, Waterperry House, Waterperry church, Waterperry Horticultural Centre and Tea Rooms can all be visited. Turn left across the bridge to the house and car park.

Day Nine

WATERPERRY TO HENTON

Waterperry GR 628064 to Henton GR 760031

The route is across the low-lying land of the valley of the River Thame; we cross it by its ancient bridges. Thame is the lively market-town reached half-way through the day. From there we continue on flat land to Henton, with the scarp slope of the Chiltern Hills rising sharply in front of us.

Distance: 11.1 miles (17.5 km).

Maps: Explorer 180 – Oxford, Witney and Woodstock.
Explorer 181 – Chiltern Hills North.
Landranger 165 – Aylesbury and Leighton Buzzard area.

Buses: Thame Bus links to Oxford and High Wycombe – Tel: 08450 788788
National Express – Tel: 0990 808080.

Rail: Chiltern Railways Company – local station, Haddenham, links to Birmingham and London – Tel: 01494 443497.

Taxis: Thame   • Dencars – Tel: 01844873105.
                   • Thame Taxis – Tel: 01844 215000/216161.
                   • Premier Cars – Tel: 01844 217700/216633.

Car Parking: Waterperry – in the Horticultural Centre overflow car park, on the right, just inside the garden entrance.
Henton – on the wide verges west of the Peacock Hotel.

Accommodation/Public Houses/Refreshments:
Shabbington   • The Old Fishermans PH – Tel: 01844 201247.
Thame   • Tourist Office – Tel: 01844 212834 for comprehensive list of information for the Thame area.
                • Several PHs and cafés along High Street and Upper High Street.

Towersey   • The Three Horseshoes PH – Tel: 01844 212322.
Henton   • Peacock Hotel – Tel: 01844 353519.
Bledlow   • Cross Lanes Cottage B&B – Tel: 01844 345337.
            (1 mile from route: recommended access by footpath
            via Skittle Green rather than along busy B4009)
            • The Lions of Bledlow PH – Tel: 01844 343345.

From the **Waterperry** Horticultural Centre car park, circle around the edge of the garden away from Waterperry House (SW) to cross the cattle-grid bridge, turn left, and continue along this bridleway. On reaching a gate, turn left, then right, to continue on the track along the right side of the brook, with the water meadows on either side. This path ends at Bow Bridge over the River Thame, past the 18th century Waterstock Mill. Immediately after leaving the mill, and opposite the entrance to the garages in the driveway, turn left over a stile. Bear half-left across a paddock, to another stile in the far fence. Cross the track and through a wrought-iron kissing gate. Turn left along the road to **Waterstock** village. The church has a genealogy window of 45 shields and a modern Millennium window. Walk along the

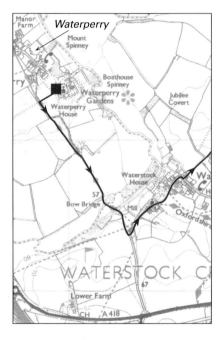

village street, ignoring the Oxfordshire Way footpath sign on the right-hand side. The building with the curiously shaped roof near the entrance of Waterstock House is the Pump House which used to provide water for the house and some of the villagers until a mains supply was established in 1951. When the road turns right, turn left along the track before the war memorial cross. Walk on this track, through a gate, to the group of willow trees on the right. Continue in the same direction (NE 048°) and aim to the left (NW) side of two solitary hedgerow trees ahead towards a stile. The farmer has cleared this path, though the right of way on the map is a little further north west. Go over the stile into the next field and aim for the stone river bridge by bearing further right (E 064°) to near the corner of the right-hand side field hedge.

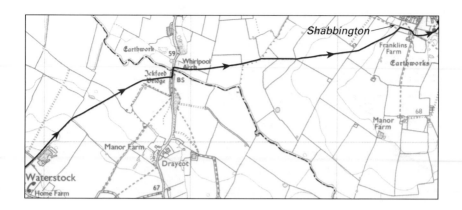

On approaching the road, aim to the right of the white railings. A stile leads out onto the road, then turn left. The bridge over the River Thame is the medieval Ickford Bridge. Exactly on the boundary, within a refuge on the right side of the bridge, there are tablets which say '1685 Here Ends the County of Oxon' and 'Here Begineth the County of Bucks 1685'.

Once over the bridge, turn right on the footpath just before the northernmost arch of the bridge, known as Whirlpool Arch. In this flood-meadow, go over the concrete bridge, cross the stile, then go ahead to the end of the narrow riverside field. Cross the second stile (not where it is expected from the map), bear left away from the river across the next field (E 069°) to a hedgerow with tall willow trees in it. Cross the foot-bridge and walk on the left side of the hedge. Cross right over another bridge onto a well-marked footpath through three fields in the direction (088°) of **Shabbington** church at the right (S) end of the village. This is the alluvial flood-plain of the River Thame. Near the corner of the third field, cross a track to a stile on the right side of a long timber barn. Cross the stile and bridge, and bear diagonally left (063°) to the north-east corner of the next field. At a stile by a jump, enter a small paddock, cross another stile and go out by the stile at a steel gate. Turn right onto the road, then almost immediately left, over a stile and bear left across the field to the stile into the churchyard. On looking back to your right at the field, the grassy bumps are the remains of the house platforms of a deserted medieval village. The

Engraving on Ickford Bridge

church is on the edge of the village, but in medieval times, it would have been at the centre. Shabbington church has some herring-bone masonry in the North walls dating from the end of the Norman period (1160).

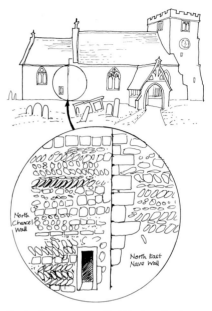

The plan of the church is a rare example of an unaltered (two cell) church, originating from the earlier Saxon plans, and was rather old fashioned even when it was built!

Access Point: Shabbington, 3.1 miles. Telephone, post office and stores. Limited parking on road near post office. GR 667069.

Herring bone masonry, Shabbington church

Go out of the churchyard and cross the road onto the footpath that forms part of the Thame Valley Walk. Walk parallel to the river (the county boundary) to the middle of the hedge at the end of the first field. Cross a stile and bear left on the downhill side of some stables to continue along the left side of the hedge to a second stile, and then along the right edge of a large field. This has more remains of ridge

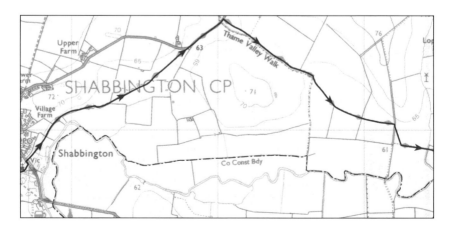

and furrow ploughing and contrasts with the flat water-meadows by the river, which were too wet for ploughing. At the next stile, go through an enclosure hedge and ditch, and bear diagonally left along the field (NE 060°) to the right of a brick barn with a black roof. At the gate, enter another field and bear diagonally right towards some buildings on the far side of the hedge and the road. This field has a perfect example of ridge and furrow ploughing. It is from here that we have our first view of the Chiltern Hills, at the foot of which is our day's destination, Henton. At the road gate turn right, and in 350 yards turn right along the left side of a ditch and a hedge. Lady's smock (cuckoo flower) and water crowfoot were growing when we walked through in April, and curlew were calling from the damp water meadows in June. Follow this footpath towards the market-town of **Thame** and the square tower of its church (SE 125°). Keep to the left side of the hedge but in an L-shaped field where the hedge ends, bear further right (145°) by a waymark post, to pass by the end of a hedge on the far side of the field After another field, cross a track to go ahead through another field to a stile on the far side (E 105°) where there is another track. Climb a stile into a field, turn right and walk around the field perimeter, across another stile, and along the right side of a barbed-wire fence. Cross a stile and walk east along the right side of the hedge for two fields keeping parallel to the Thame bypass. On joining the former Thame road, turn right, cross the bypass with care, and go over a bridge with several flood arches (used in the days when the River Thame flooded). Pass the county boundary marker into **Oxfordshire**.

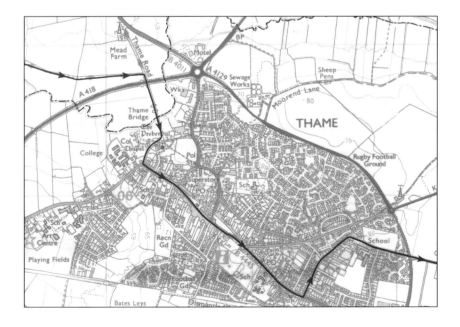

Boundary marker over the River Thame

Access Point: Thame Church, 6.1 miles. GR 704063.

Turn right past Thame church. On reaching the High Street, turn left. There is a choice of hotels and public houses here. We chose the Coffee Pot on the left side of the Buttermarket.

Continue along the High Street, then where the road divides, take the road B445 marked Chinnor, past the *Shell* garage and turn left along Queen's Road marked to the 'Tennis and Bowls Club'. Walk past Kings Road which joins from the left to a road signed 'Towersey Road – No Through Road', which goes right, past Lord Williams' School. Cross the Thame bypass and continue in the same direction to the village of **Towersey**. Again the element *ey* in the name indicates that the village was on an island in former times. It is worth making a diversion to see the church with its 13th-century lancet windows. Although the most direct route to Henton is straight ahead along Manor Road, to explore the village, turn right on the Chinnor road for 50 yards to the Three Horseshoes public house.

Thame Market Place

Thame is an ancient market-town. It originated from its site by the river:
the church was rebuilt in the 15th century. It is a church with a fine marble
monument of Lord Williams and his wife. By its side is the Prebendal, the medieval
residence of a canon of Lincoln. It was the Bishop of Lincoln in the 12th century
who created the boat-shaped market area, including the butter and corn market.
Cattle markets and a Tuesday street market are still held. It was during Thame's
economic depression in 1835 that the workhouse (now Rycotewood College) was
built. A guide to many of the buildings in Thame is available from the Tourist
Information Centre.

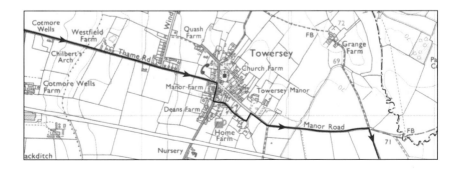

Access Point: Towersey, 8.5 miles. Telephone. GR 735052.

Turn left onto a footpath beside the Three Horseshoes pub and continue south-east, ignoring the footpath sign to the left. Cross a narrow field with a pond in it, along a small green lane ahead, and turn left (NE) down a drive to join Manor Road. Turn right along the road for 0.75 miles, until it ends at a fingerpost signed 'Henton 2 miles'. Turn right along a footpath/farm road, across the disused railway, now the Phoenix Trail for cyclists, past the right side of Penn Farm and onwards south-east to New Close Farm. Continue south past the timbered barns and farmhouse. Turn left, then, when the track turns south again, ignore the footpath sign to the left, and continue between thick hedges and beside an ancient woodland bank on your left. Join a track and continue to New Close Farm Road. Where a bridleway joins from the right, go straight ahead, then continue to **Henton** village. The Peacock Inn is to the left (N), a telephone box is to the right. There are wide verges for parking.

Day Ten
HENTON TO NORTHEND

Henton GR 760031 to Northend GR 735925

This is a day spent in glorious beechwoods in an Area of Outstanding Natural Beauty. The trees, originally planted for the furniture industry, offer recreation amongst typical chalk downland and woodland fauna and flora. 100 miles of the route are achieved north of Sprigs Alley. This area is sparsely populated, so take plenty of food and water.

Distance: 12.6 miles (20.2 km), short cut 10.6 miles (17 km).

Maps: Explorer 181 – Chiltern Hills North.
Explorer 171 – Chiltern Hills West.

Taxis: Northend • Mr B. Shirfield – Tel: 01491 638358, can provide minibus.
• Henley-on-Thames Chiltern Taxis – Tel: 01491 577888.
• County Cars – Tel: 01491 579696.
• Harris Taxis – Tel: 01491 577036.
• Talbot Taxis – Tel: 01491 574222.

Car Parking: Henton – on the wide grass verges west of the Peacock Hotel.
Northend – edge of the village green, near the pond.

Accommodation/Public Houses/Refreshments:
None on route, nearest pub and B&Bs are:
Bennett End • The Three Horseshoes PH – Tel: 01494 483273. (0.4 miles from route E of Crowell Wood).
Watlington • Woodgate Orchard Cottage B&B, Howe Road – Tel: 01491 612675. (3.25 miles from Northend but collection service offered).
Stonor • White Pond Farm (GR736893) – Tel: 01491 638224. Fax: 01491 638428. (2.5 miles by road, or 3.1 miles further on along route, see Day 11).

Pishill (NB this hamlet is 0.4 miles away from Day 11 route).
- Orchard House (GR 726900) – Tel: 01491 638351. (4.5 miles from Northend by road, or 3.5 miles further along Day 11 route).
- Pishill Bank Farm (GR 723899) – Tel: 01491 638601. Distances from route as above.

Henley-on-Thames Tourist Information Office for full list of local accommodation – Tel: 01491 578034.

From near Home Farm at the north end of **Henton**, walk south, passing the telephone box.

On passing College Farm on the right, note the Magdalen College crest of white lilies in the bricks of the front wall. There is a saying that you could walk from Oxford to London on Magdalen College ground, so extensive was the land owned by this Oxford college! Much of the land around Henton was sold in the 1940s.

Magdalen College crest, Henton

In winter, a cross is visible in the scarp slope of the Chilterns ahead. This is Bledlow Cross, a simple Greek cross cut in chalk on Wain Hill. The date is unknown but the earliest description of it was made in 1827. At the road junction, turn right, then almost immediately left over a stile signed 'Wainhill', and up the right side of a hedge. We saw small tortoiseshell butterflies here in June. Cross the Chinnor and Princes Risborough railway line which has a recreational steam-engine (Tel: 01844 353535). Continue (175°) up through a paddock towards a large brick house with a Dutch gable ('Whitebeam'). Keep straight on over stiles uphill through four further paddocks ignoring footpaths to the left and right, and continue uphill through a small gate, into the garden of 'Whitebeam'. Turn left onto the stony track beyond it. Pass the next house, then bear right to start climbing up a narrow path with a hedge on the left and a wooden paling fence on the right. The chalk of the Chiltern Hills is at the surface. Turn right at the next brick house, past the gates of Wainhill Cottage, and immediately left following the bridleway uphill (and not the Icknield Way or the

Ridgeway). This is the county boundary, with Buckinghamshire to the left and Oxfordshire to the right. It is a sunken way with indicators of ancient woodland, such as primroses, woodruff, ferns and dog's mercury. The BBOWT nature reserve notice-board describes the chalk pits and explains that these large hollows were dug in the early modern period (16th–17th century) by local farmers who used the chalk to lime the fields to make the soil less acid.

The track broadens out to reach the top of the scarp slope, where there is a bench with extensive views to the north over the Aylesbury Vale. There are large juniper trees on the right, the berries of which are used to make gin. Yellow and brown banded snails can be found here, typical of a chalk downland habitat. The walk continues through an area of planted ash trees with their autumn bunches of seeds called 'keys'.

Follow the path until it joins a metalled road, turn left, through a car park (for BBOWT reserve visitors), then right (205°) alongside Hill Top cottages and 'Owls Wood' to the left.

Access Point: BBOWT car park,
2.0 miles. GR 767003.

At the end of Hill Top Lane, turn left to walk along Red Lane for half a mile. Ignore the footpath sign to Sprigs Alley on the right. Walk past the wooden clapboarded house, 'County End' on the left and the next sign to Hedgerley Wood House on the right, then, just at the corner of a sharp left-hand bend in the road, turn right (SE) along the county boundary.

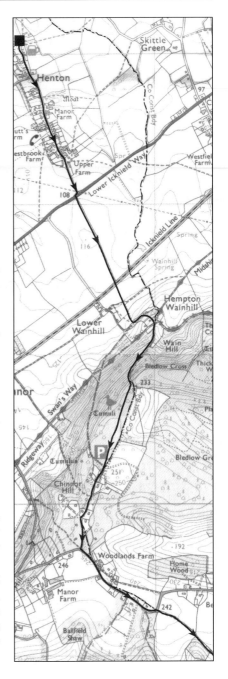

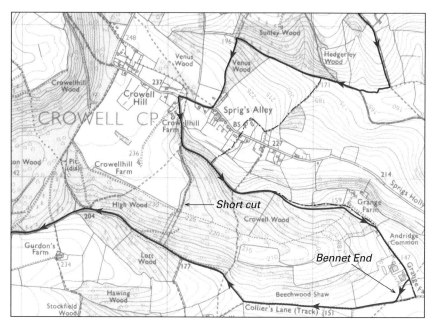

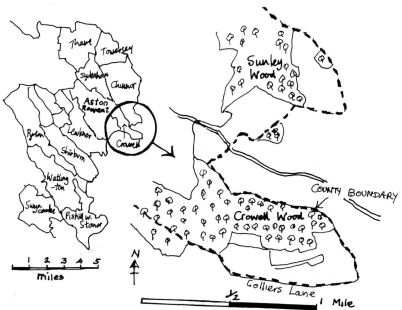

County boundary, north of Stokenchurch

The reason for making this detour is that the county boundary has long extensions or 'tongues' into woodland at right angles up the slope from the lowlands. The boundary dates back to the demarcations of the ancient woodland rights giving the Anglo-Saxon villagers both some low, arable land and some high, wooded land for timber, poles and fire-wood. The villagers drove their pigs up to the forests to exercise their rights of pannage (the fattening of domestic pigs on acorns and beech mast).

B.M. MS. Roy. 2. B, VII

Medieval peasants with swine

Walk along the hedge through two gates and through a remnant of woodland. Continue along the next field keeping close to the ancient hedge, which is the county boundary. We saw red kites 'quartering' the slopes here.

Red Kites

Red kites were successfully re-introduced into this area in 1988 from Spain, with the support of the Royal Society for the Protection of Birds (RSPB) and Sir Paul Getty, a keen local contributor to wildlife conservation.

Cross a stile at the end of the field, bear left (SE 135°) through a hay meadow to a gate in the opposite corner of this rectangular field. On the other side of the gate turn sharp right, doubling back into a narrow, ancient, hedge-lined bridleway. There is hazel coppicing on either side and these trees make a green tunnel. Continue on in the same direction to walk along the left-hand (S) edge of Sunley Wood where we saw a variety of large fungi.

Turn left up to the edge of Venus Wood. It is here that the 100 mile point is reached (GR 765989). Pass Pond Farm on the right, then at the road through Sprigs Alley, turn right. Walk along the road until you come to a concrete track leading left, sign-posted 'Crowell Hill Farm'. Almost immediately after entering the farm entrance, descend by a narrow, tree-covered bridleway left of the concrete track leading to the farm buildings. This is a sunken way, but there is a footpath to the right above it, which makes easier walking in wet weather. This is a good example of how one sunken way becomes disused and a new, drier one is formed further up the slope. At the junction of the footpaths, turn sharp left, to walk along in the bottom of a valley with Crowell Wood to the right (125°). Very soon, the county boundary joins our path from along the first hedgeline on the left edge of the wood. Continue to walk along the boundary.

If you wish to take a short-cut (reducing the route by 2 miles), it is possible to walk straight across at the junction of the tracks (GR 761983), though this misses out the county boundary line.
Keep to the edge of the wood, then follow the bridleway. When the wood extends to the right, keep going down the stony path at right angles to the slope. Carry on past a forestry track, down to the county boundary which is in the bottom of the valley. Turn right and rejoin the Seven Shires Way at GR 760975.

This path follows the northern perimeter of one of the 'tongues' of the ancient boundary demarcation for one mile, and joins a tarmac track going in the same direction. Pass Colliers Lane Farm on the right, then where the footpath (also the Chiltern Way) joins from the left, go though the gap in the hedge, cross the farmyard, go along by the wire fence, and diagonally left across the paddock to meet a stony track. Turn right (W 265°). This track is called Colliers Lane (from the days of the charcoal burning industry), it follows the southern perimeter of the 'tongue' of

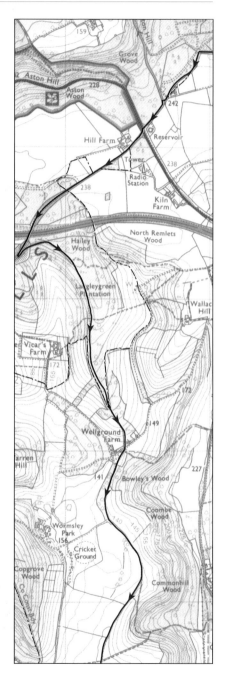

land and is bordered by ancient antlered oaks. It is the county boundary. Follow the bridleway to the fork in the track before Hallbottom Farm, bear right and continue along the county boundary in another ancient tree-covered lane. Follow the white arrows, S87, waymarks placed by the Chiltern Society in the wood along the bottom of the valley. The short-cut route (see box on page 92) joins by a downhill track on the right. Continue on the main track and then further on, where there is another dividing of the ways, bear left to take the track along the edge of the wood. This is still the county boundary. On meeting the road, turn left to the crossroads, then dog-leg left and right across the A40 road. The county boundary signs for Buckinghamshire and Oxfordshire are evident.

Access point: Hill Farm Road, 8.6 miles (short cut 6.6 miles). GR 745971.

Walk along the road, which is also the county boundary, to where a minor road leaves to the right. Here is a huge sarsen stone. (This can be partially hidden by nettles in summer).

Sarsen stones are boulders, the remnants of a hard siliceous (quartz) sandstone crust that once overlay the chalk hills. Because these stones were so hard and difficult to move, they made good markers or signs of ancient boundaries. Whether this one has simply been dragged to the edge of the field by farm machinery or was an ancient boundary stone, we do not know. There are other good examples at Ashdown House on Day 16.

Sarsen Stone, north of Stokenchurch

Continue along the road, cross the motorway (M40) bridge to a footpath sign on the left side, indicating a path that doubles back left on the other side of the roadside metal barrier. We saw pyramidal orchids and our first marbled white butterfly of the summer here. Descend the hill into the **Wormsley Estate** (also an English Nature reserve). Keeping high on the slope (160°), cross the junction of four paths then slowly descend the side of a deep valley to the right. The planting of beech trees can be seen to replace those blown down in the October gales of 1987. Wild privet, honeysuckle, St John's wort and clustered bellflower were all growing here. The county boundary is to the right. On arriving at the private road near Wellground Farm, turn right and take the tarmac bridleway (S 205°) signpost-

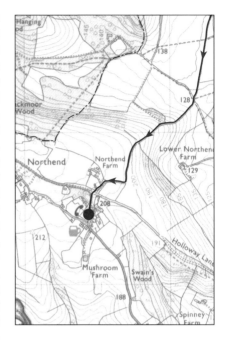

ed 'Wormsley'. The gates and house of Wormsley Park can be seen to the right. Where the road turns right to the cricket ground, bear left (145°) along the grassy bridleway. Where the track divides, take the right-hand path away from the woods so keeping to the bottom of the valley. Walk on past the junction marked 'S21 Wormsley Estate' and continue on the main track south to a meeting of five ways at the bottom of a hill.

The sarsen stones at the junction could have formerly been used as 'mere stones', (marker stones of a man's property or boundary). Take the bridleway south-west that climbs up the hill and into an embanked tree-lined way. This is an ancient path as indicated by the old coppiced beech and hazel trees. This coppicing of hazel trees makes it an ideal habitat for doormice. Fallow, roe and muntjac deer can be seen occasionally in these Chiltern woods. Bear left where the stony track meets a tarmac lane. It is worth turning to look back to admire the view of this dry valley in the chalk hills.

Leave the Wormsley Estate by a pair of sarsen stones and the gate leading to the road, to arrive on the edge of the village of **Northend**. The name Northend refers to the original scattered forest settlement on the edge of the woods (cf. Southend, a village 2.5 miles south-east of Northend). Cross the road, taking the sign straight ahead to Turville Heath and Fingest. Pass the pond to the right, and onto the wide village green where there is a telephone. N.B. The pub is now closed.

Day Eleven

NORTHEND TO
HENLEY-ON-THAMES

Northend GR 735925 to Henley-on-Thames GR 766822

A day of mainly gradual descent through woodland and open fields, travelling through the graciousness of Stonor and Henley Parks to meet the boundary at the River Thames.

Distance: 11 miles (17.2 km).

Maps: Explorer 171 – Chiltern Hills West, Henley-on-Thames & Wallingford.
Landranger – 175 Reading & Windsor, Henley-on-Thames & Bracknell.

Transport: Hourly buses and trains from Henley to London, Oxford, Reading and High Wycombe.

Taxis: Northend
• Mr B. Shirfield – Tel: 01491 638358, minibus can be provided.

Middle Assendon
• Shalna Chauffeur Hire – Tel: 01491 575754/ 07850 933700.

Henley on Thames
• County Cars – Tel: 01491 579696.
• Harris Taxis – Tel: 01491 577036.

Car Parking: Northend – on the edge of the village green, near the pond.
Henley-on-Thames – Mill Meadows car park, fee payable.

Accommodation/Public Houses/Refreshments:
Pishill
• Crown Inn – Tel: 01491 638364.
(GR 725900. 0.5 miles from route).
For B&B accommodation, see Day 10.

Stonor
• White Pond Farm B&B – Tel: 01491 638224.
• The Stonor Arms – Tel: 01491 638866.

Fawley Bottom
• Jackson's Farm – Tel: 01491 575330.
(GR 749870. 1 mile from route).

Middle Assendon
• Rainbow Inn – Tel: 01491 574879.

Lower Assendon
- Park View Farm – Tel: 01491 414232. (GR 745847. 0.6 miles from route).
- Orchard Dene Cottage – Tel: 01491 575490. (0.6 miles from route).

Henley-on-Thames
- Old White Horse B&B, 100, Northfield End – Tel: 01491 575763.
- 3 Western Road B&B – Tel: 01491 573468.
- Little White Hart – Tel: 01491 574145.
- Swiss Farm International Camping – Tel: 01491 573419.

Henley on Thames Tourist Information Office – Tel: 01491 578034 for full accommodation list. There is a plentiful supply of teashops in Henley.

Northend village Hall

From Northend village green, walk in front of the flint-built village hall and along a narrow road leading right (NW) for 600 yards, to turn left into an enclosed path between houses (also part of the Chiltern Way, a 133 mile circular walk round the Chilterns). Go over a stile into a field, and bear left to go over another stile and descend to meet the bridleway in the bottom of the hollow. Turn left down the dry valley following the county boundary with Oxfordshire to the right and Buckinghamshire to the left. Enter a wood carpeted by the wood brome grass. At the crossroads of the tracks, turn left and follow the track along the county boundary for nearly two miles keeping straight on in the base of the valley following the woodland edge.

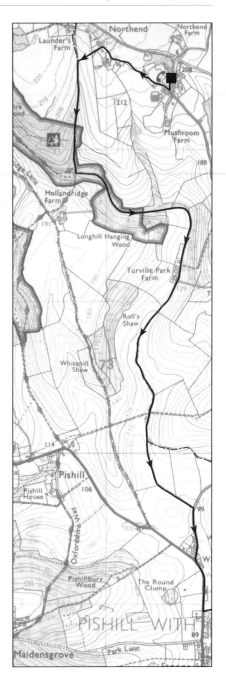

We saw speckled wood butterflies here, and there were musk mallows in flower with deeply-cut leaves producing a fine tracery of green, altogether a much more delicate plant than the common mallow. This is red kite country; there were several wheeling overhead at Turville Park Farm as we passed by.

Walk on beside a fine avenue of planted ash trees. This avenue continues as a mature, mixed line of mostly oak, ash and beech trees forming the curving course of the county boundary in the bottom of the valley. Marjoram, field scabious, hairy mint and St John's wort were growing along the hedgerow on the left. At the end of the track, turn right along the road by the edge of the Stonor

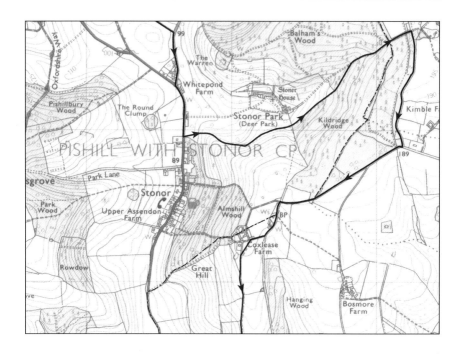

estate, past White Pond Farm (B&B) and branch left on meeting the wider road. The high iron railing on the left is the deer fence erected in 1891 when the deer-park was established. Walk with care along this narrow road past the main entrance of Stonor Park to reach the kissing gate in the iron railings 150 yards further on.

Access point: Stonor, 3 miles. Pub, telephone. GR 737886.

   Turn left away from the road up the footpath marked 'Chiltern Way'. Climb up the slope, enjoying the fine views of Stonor Park and House on the left.

At the top of the slope in the open land, there are large leafy plants with dark purple flowers and green fruit in July. This is deadly nightshade, a woodland plant which would have established itself in the shade of the woods before many of the trees were blown down in the October 1987 gales. The fruit goes a glossy-black colour later summer and the whole plant is extremely poisonous as its name suggests. Stinking iris, another woodland species, can be found further along the track just as the woodland is reached. There is a large herd of fallow deer in the park which you may glimpse if lucky.

Stonor House and Park

This name originates from the Old English word *stanora* meaning 'at the stones', referring to the huge sarsen stones that were here in the 9th century. The ring of stones near the house is of recently gathered sarsens and is a modern folly. The estate has belonged to the Stonor family since the 12th century. The medieval house has an Elizabethan brick facade and the chapel is 14th century. House open April–Sept, Weds (July & Aug only) & Sun 2–5.30pm. Tea room. Admission £4.50 – Tel: 01491 638587.

Climb on up the slope through the woods, and about 200 yards before reaching the road, there is a half-buried sarsen stone in the path. This stone is likely to be a marker for the county boundary, which we cross here.

On reaching the top of the wooded slope, where a track enters on the left, there were until recently, two large, round, rusty iron bins. These were remnants from the charcoal burning industry. The Stonor estate supplied charcoal from these woods which was used by Courtaulds in the manufacture of nylon in the 1950s.

Turn right to walk along the minor road just past the brick and flint estate cottages. There are sweet or Spanish chestnut trees in the bank to the right. These trees were first introduced from Spain and have long male catkins in spring and a shiny casing to the chestnuts in autumn. The woodland edge here is rich in other tree species including old Scots pine, hazel, hawthorn, holly, oak, ash, field maple, wild cherry and honeysuckle, again indicating an ancient wood.

Turn right at the road junction from where there are extensive views to the left across the valley of the River Thames. An avenue of beech trees on the right marks the county boundary as it joins the road at an oblique angle just before a clump of trees to the left which marks a tumulus known as the King's Barrow. Turn left at the sharp corner further on, ignoring the footpath ahead to Stonor. The county boundary continues to follow the road, leaving it just before the first cottage. We could find no sign of the boundary post marked BP on the map (see page 98). Keep on the road. At the old oak tree, turn right onto the concrete track to Coxleaze Farm. At the farmhouse gates and cattle grid, keep left (S) along the track. Further on there are good views of the Assendon Valley to the right. The county boundary follows the valley bottom.

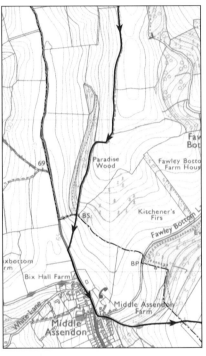

On walking down the path for 0.75 miles, there is a bank (a lynchet) where the medieval farmers ploughed along the contours of the slope (see also Day 3). It is rich with flowers and grasses: in July, knapweed, poppies, field scabious, restharrow and marjoram were all attracting a wide variety of bees and butterflies, including marbled whites and common blues. We saw the delightful fragrant orchid, pale toadflax, goatsbeard and musk (or nodding) thistle on this bank.

On reaching a large field ahead, turn right along the left-hand side of the hedge. Walk down the slope and over the stile into Paradise Wood, an ancient wood of coppiced hazel trees. Turn left to follow a narrow path on the left, uphill-side of the wood and on leaving it at the far end, turn half-right. Here the county boundary is crossed, but again we could find no evidence of the boundary stone (BS) marked on the map. The boundary shifts eastwards to avoid dividing the village ahead and was originally likely to have been an estate boundary. Walk down across the middle of a field (200°) to a wide road gateway. Turn left where, in June, common mallow and convolvulus (lesser bindweed) with its stripey pink-and-white flowers, grow on the road banks. This road leads into **Middle Assendon**.

Access point: Middle Assendon, 8 miles. Pub, telephone, taxi. GR 739857.

By the pub, bear away left from the main road, passing a water-worn sarsen stone and four beautiful lime trees on the small triangular green. Walk for 100 yards, then turn right behind the village houses to follow the Oxfordshire Way up the slope on a green lane.

On leaving the wood at the top, bear left on a well marked-footpath across the field. We saw the unusual plant, fumitory, with its fine feathery leaves and multiple purplish-red flowers, visible from May to September. We recommend turning

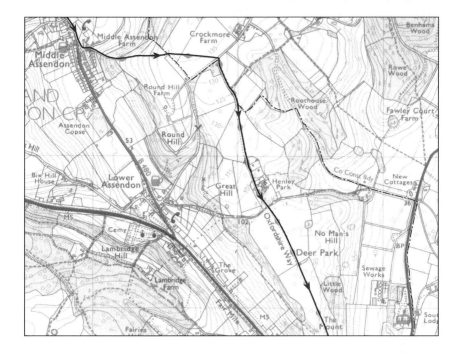

around to admire the view. To the right (N), the county boundary runs parallel to the village, one field away from the road. There are several large trees in this multi-specied hedge. At the top of the field go through the hedge, left of the wooden paddock fence. Turn right on the other side of the hedge and walk between railings to a stile. Walk across the field to a stile in the hedge. Cross the road and continue on the same path as the Oxfordshire Way. Walk along the stony track with lime trees on the right. This is the start of Henley Park which was established here in the Middle Ages. We were lucky to see a roe deer on the woodland edge. Walk past the house of Henley Park with its fine redwood trees and through a wooden gate into the next field past a splendidly large Cedar of

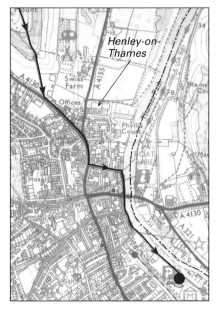

Lebanon. Go through an iron kissing gate, through a pig farm and across the field, continuing to walk (SE) downhill. Walk through another iron kissing gate into the wood with beech trees planted in avenues and box bushes beneath. Keep moving downhill towards the road. Turn left here and walk along the Fairmile road for 400 yards to a roundabout. Continue ahead into the town of **Henley-on-Thames**. At Asquith's Teddy Bear shop, turn left into New Street past Brakspear's Brewery. At Church Avenue, leading right to the almshouses and chantry house, is a chamfered corner in brick, moulded just for the same purpose as in the stone houses described in Day 5. At the River Thames, turn right to enjoy the riverside walk towards the fine bridge and the Red Lion Hotel. Cross Hart Street at the traffic lights to follow the river bank for 600 yards. At the entrance of the Mill/Marsh Meadow, turn right through the children's play area to return to the car park.

River and Rowing Museum - Tel: 01491 415600.
Brakspear's Brewery, New Street - Tel: 01491 570200.
Hobbs Boat Hire - Tel: 01491 572035.

Henley-on-Thames

This lively and attractive riverside town is famous for its regatta. It has a gracious 18th century bridge. Many timber-framed houses remain, together with an early theatre and a cigar-shaped market place. Places of interest to visit include: Brakspear's Brewery and the interactive River and Rowing Museum. Here you can test your own rowing prowess, or try to balance in a make-believe racing boat or just listen to music, poetry and literature inspired by the River Thames. Real boats can be hired!

Henley River and Rowing Museum

Day Twelve

HENLEY-ON-THAMES TO TILEHURST

Henley-on-Thames GR 766822 to Tilehurst GR 675752

A day of riverside walking, much of it following the Thames Path, pleasing at any time of the year, with quiet stretches in between the busy river fronts of Reading and Caversham. We pass where Oscar Wilde was imprisoned, and follow the path made by barge horses in times when much cargo was water-borne. We reach the sixth shire, Berkshire.

Distance: 12.4 miles (21 km).

Maps: Explorer 171 – Chiltern Hills West, Henley-on-Thames and Wallingford.
Explorer 159 – Reading, Wokingham and Pangbourne (optional extra map).
Landranger 175 – Reading, Windsor and surrounding area.

Transport: Tilehurst railway station – on main London/Oxford line
Henley station on branch line from Twyford.
Bus – Ridgeway Explorer stops at Reading railway station & Roebuck Hotel, Tilehurst. (Summer service only)
Contact: Stagecoach, Swindon & District – Tel: 01793 522243.

Taxis: Reading   • Central Cars – Tel: 0118 9874444.
Caversham   • 500 Cars – Tel: 0118 9500501/9582582.
Tilehurst   • First City – Tel: 0118 9413434.

Car Parking: Henley-on-Thames – Mill Meadows car park, fee payable.
Tilehurst railway station car park, or in one of the roads on the hill opposite.

Public Houses/Accommodation/Refreshments:
Lower Shiplake   • Baskerville Arms – Tel: 0118 9403332.
  • Kingsley, 1 Crowell Road, B&B – Tel: 0118 9493626.
Sonning   • Bull Inn – Tel: 0118 9693901.
  • Great House Hotel – Tel: 0118 9692277.
  • French Horn Hotel – Tel: 0118 9692204.
  • The Teacosy – Tel: 0118 9698178.

Reading	• Abbey House Hotel, 118 Connaught Road – Tel: 0118 9569299.
	• Berkeley Guest House, 32 Berkley Avenue – Tel: 0118 9595699.
	• Rainbow Corner Hotel, 132 Caversham Road – Tel: 0118 9588140.
	• Gorge Cafe – Tel: 0118 9503446.
Caversham	• Pipers Riverside PH – Tel: 0118 9484573 (includes Thai River Restaurant).
Tilehurst	• Roebuck Hotel, Oxford Road – Tel: 0118 9427517.
	• Warren Dene Hotel, 1017 Oxford Road – Tel: 0118 9422556.

For wider choice of accommodation, see Thames Path Companion – Tel: 01865 810224.

From **Henley-on-Thames** walk upstream (SE) beside the River Thames on the Thames Path, a 180 mile long route which goes from the river source west of Lechlade to the Thames Barrier in London. Here the Thames forms the county boundary: Oxfordshire (near bank) and Berkshire (far bank). Walk on the former towpath and turn left to cross over to Marsh Lock island by a pair of long, wooden horse-bridges.

Wooden Horse Bridges, Henley-on-Thames

Mills, Marshes and Locks

The river would have had several mills and flash-locks in the 15th century. A flash-lock was a primitive way of navigating from an upper to a lower reach of a river. A weir with a central gate was built across the river and the water ponded back. The boat was stationed above the gate. When this was opened, the 'flash', (rush of water), carried the boat through. In the opposite direction, a winch was used to drag the boat through the gap. The flash-lock was replaced by the pound-lock in the 17th century. This is a version of lock in which the boat is moved up and down between two gates and is the one we now use for canal traffic.

There were probably grain mills here by 1790: two mills on the far bank, a corn and paper mill on the near bank and a flash-lock in the centre of the river. Today's pound-lock remains in the middle of the channel, with the now redundant mill streams flowing past on either side. The pair of horse-bridges had to be built to provide a bypass around the mill on the west side because the mill blocked the towpath. Wargrave Marsh is a long lowland area enclosed by the main channel of the Thames and Hennerton Backwater: Marsh Lock refers to this land being liable to flooding.

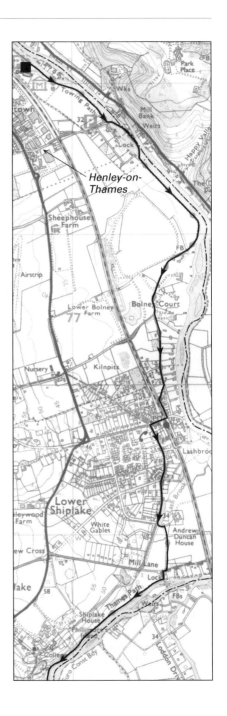

Walk on upstream along a narrow footpath. Where the meadow begins, on the right by the wooden barrier, there is an iron stud marked 'Henley Borough Boundary 1908'. In the meadow, 300 yards on is another iron stud, this one put there to mark the fourteen-foot width of the towing path in the days of horse-drawn barges. The bank has since been eroded, so that this stud is now only about three feet from the river bank.

On looking across to the opposite bank, there is the ornately gabled lodge of Park Place. Just beyond it, the drive to the main house passes under a large arched bridge, called the Cyclopic Bridge, which carries the A321 from Twyford to Henley. This bridge was built in the 1780s of huge stones brought here from fourteen counties. At the end of this meadow it is necessary to leave the river for a while, so cross the concrete bridge into a narrow path between fences which joins a drive. At the end of the drive fork left, and walk about 400 yards along the road lined with sweet chestnut trees. We saw the aptly named lawyer's wig fungus in the shade of the trees in the gardens. At Rivermead House, take a footpath, also the Thames Path, to bear right to walk between hedges. *Do not* cross the Henley branch railway line but take the footpath along the left-hand side. At the end of the footpath turn right across the railway at **Shiplake** station.

Access Point: Lower Shiplake Railway Station, 2 miles. Pub, telephone, shop. GR 776797.

At the crossroads ahead, continue left along Mill Road for 0.5 of a mile past the cottages of **Lashbrook**. Ignore the first footpath sign to the left. The white, boarded, barn-like building on the left is Lashbrook Chapel. Continue walking out of the village and turn left along a minor road signposted to Lashbrook Nursing Home. Immediately after crossing the bridge, turn right down wooden steps, over a stile, and cross to the left-hand corner of the field. It is worth looking back to where you entered, as there is a multi-arched bridge, built to carry the road when the River Thames floods these meadows.

Climb the stile, then turn right along the field edge to the lane by Mill House. Turn right at this track, then immediately left on a fenced path leading to **Shiplake Lock**. A small kiosk sells drinks and confectionery here. *Do not* cross the footbridge, but turn right over a stile onto the towing path, walking upstream beside the river on its west bank and under some ancient plane trees. Shiplake College and **Shiplake** village, a group of cottages on the chalk bluff, stand above the river.

Flood arches, Lashbrook

Shiplake church

Shiplake church can be reached by a footpath which leaves the Thames Path just before the wooden footbridge on the towpath, and goes steeply upwards behind the boathouse. The church was restored in the Victorian era but contains some beautiful 15th century French stained glass, brought from the ruined abbey of St Bastin in the city of St Omer on the French/Belgian border. Alfred Lord Tennyson was married here in 1850 and presented the vicar with a poem trusting that his life might flow:

> 'Smooth as Thames below your gates
> Thames along the silent levels
> Streaming thro' his osier'd aits'.

To continue along the towpath, go over the bridge in front of the Shiplake College boathouse.

This part of the path passes under large willow trees where pink Himalayan balsam was growing in September. In November alder trees had their black cones and early purplish catkins, and a 'charm' of fifty or more goldfinches were feeding on thistle seeds among the rough grassland on the bank. The river twists around the small islands called The Lynch, Hallsmead Ait and Buck Ait. An *ait* or *eyot* is an Anglo-Saxon word for a small isle.

At a division of the path, keep left along the riverside path to reach **Sonning** where there is a fine 18th century bridge which has eleven arches to span the three channels of the Thames and a flood plaque dated 1894. Sonning Mill stands hidden by trees in the centre channel. Cross the bridge, past the county boundary marker O/B in the bridge wall over the middle of the river, and turn right to walk along the east bank. We are now in **Berkshire**, the sixth shire reached on the Seven Shires Way. Sonning village has many timber-framed and Georgian houses. There are two hotels and one pub. To reach The Bull pub, walk along the east bank, to turn left (E) to take the path through the churchyard. This churchyard wall is made of Tudor bricks, a reminder of the palace of the Bishops of Salisbury which once stood at Sonning; now Blue Coat School is on the site.

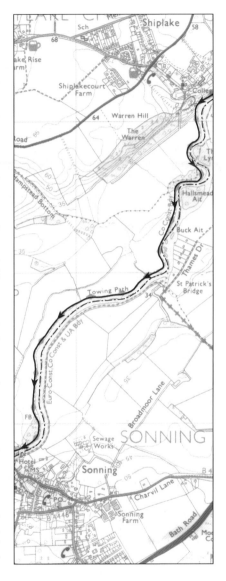

Access Point: Sonning Church, 5.5 miles. Telephone, shops and cafes. GR 755755.

To continue along the east bank, walk past Sonning Lock. This doubles as a salmon leap, a sign that the river is now sufficiently unpolluted that salmon can thrive here once again. Walk on to where water-meadows stretch down to the river, the buildings and gasometers of Reading are far from the riverbank. The River Kennet enters from the south. Cross over the footbridge known as 'the Horseshoe Bridge'.

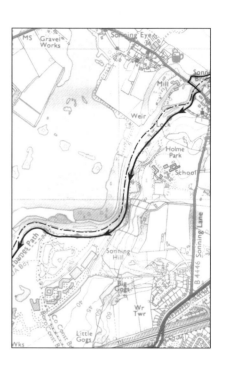

Horseshoe Bridge

The long, gentle up and down slopes of the bridge were designed for the towing horses. Shallow steps now replace the iron treads that prevented the horses slipping. David Sharp, in his *Thames Path Guide*, reports how 'the locals tell how the horses got up speed as they approached this point so that the barges would carry across the Kennet entry without assistance'. There is a large Thames barge moored on the opposite bank, giving an idea of the weight that these horses would have had to tow.

It is 500 yards west from the bridge that the county boundary turns north around the perimeter of **Caversham**. The path passes very near the centre of **Reading**. We passed people carrying bags of shopping from the nearby supermarket who were using the towpath as the quick way home.

Keeping by the river bank, the way opens into another large water-meadow which joins with Kings Meadow on the left, a rural part of Reading. The crenellations of Reading jail can be seen, where Oscar Wilde was imprisoned in 1895, being sentenced to two years of hard labour for his homosexual practices. We saw herons here in November. This approach is remarkably quiet, with sensitive housing development on the opposite bank.

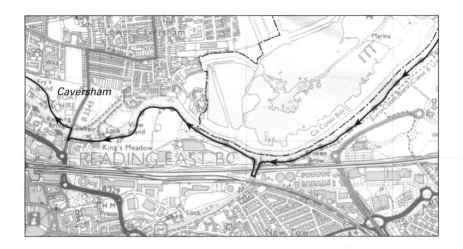

The Origin of Reading

'Readas town' originates from about 600 AD when Saxon migrants sailed up the Thames and settled beside the River Kennet. These were the Readingas, named after their leader Reada "the red one". The town stands on a well-drained ridge, in a defensive position at the junction of the River Kennet and the River Thames. It had good communications and was the centre of a rich agricultural region. By the time of Domesday (1086), Reading was a borough, a significant trading centre in one of the most populated parts of the country. Reading Museum in the Town Hall, Blagrave Street, (Tel: 0118 9399800) tells much of Reading's rich history. (GR 716735). Open Tues–Sat 10–4, Sun & BH 11–4.

Pass Caversham lock and, at Reading bridge, divert from the route of the Thames Path to climb the stone steps and cross over the bridge to the right (N) riverside in Caversham. It is possible to stay on the south bank through Reading, but we think the north side is more pleasant with the park meeting the river. On the parapet of the bridge, there are bronze casts of the former arms of the Borough of Reading: the heads of five maidens, the centre one crowned.

Access Points:

Reading, 8.6 miles. Reading station car park is 600 yards from the route. To reach it, turn left (S) at Reading Bridge after which the car park is signed. GR 718740.

Caversham, 8.7 miles. Use Reading station car park on south bank of river. GR 718741

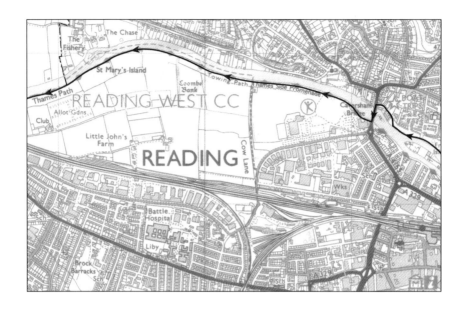

Caversham

Caversham was once the site of a major eel fishing industry. Many of the riverside communities made their living by fishing until the late 1800s. Huge wicker eel baskets were used. This example of an eel spear can be seen in the River and Rowing Museum at Henley-on-Thames (see Day 11).

Eel spear found at Caversham

Turn left through the meadow (there are public toilets on the far side), and at the war memorial bear right away from the river and behind the flats, to arrive on the road leading to Caversham Bridge. Since the traffic is busy here, turn right at The Crown on the Bridge pub, and on to the traffic lights. Cross the road, and turn left to double back over Caversham Bridge. At the south end of the bridge is an iron plaque in the wall describing the importance of this bridge as a river crossing from the 13th century onwards.

> **Caversham Bridge**
>
> A narrow, timber bridge stood here in 1231, when there was also a chapel dedicated
> to St Anne for the use of wayfarers. In the Civil War, the Parliamentarians fought
> to control it. In 1869 an iron bridge replaced the timber, and in 1926 the present
> bridge was built.

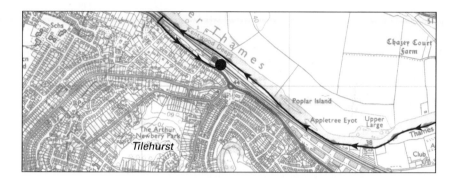

Go down the slope to the river by The Three Men in a Boat pub. There are swans
waiting to be fed here. Diced bread can be purchased as well as ice-creams from the
Riverside Tuck Shop nearby! A Victorian, stone drinking-fountain overlooks this
riverside area. Go on beside the river past a water-meadow, then pass in front of the
Reading Marine Services boatyard (shop available). Beyond here the towpath reverts
to its wild state for the last mile. Walk past wooded islands with the London/Oxford
railway line high above you. The county boundary rejoins the river from the west
side of Caversham, 300 yards after the first island, St Mary's Island. We saw a king-
fisher fishing from Appletree Eyot. Walk a mile along this narrow path until the footpath sign is reached. Turn left up a flight of stairs to cross the footbridge over the
railway north-west of **Tilehurst** railway station. It is well worth pausing to look back
at the river and to a distant view of the Chiltern Hills before reaching the A329
between Reading and Pangbourne. Turn left (E) and walk for five minutes to car
parking areas: either in Tilehurst station, Roper Road (GR 673751), or one of the other
roads on the hill opposite the station.

Day Thirteen

TILEHURST TO MOULSFORD

Tilehurst GR 675752 to Moulsford GR 590839

Further riverside walking along water-meadows between villages, with tile-hung houses and plenty of opportunities for pleasant refreshment breaks. We pass what is thought to be the oldest crossing of the Thames, and find a tree linked to the primeval 'wild wood'.

Distance: 11.2 miles (17.9 km).

Maps: Explorer 171 – Chilterns West, Henley-on-Thames and Wallingford.
Explorer 159 – Reading, Wokingham and Pangbourne.
Explorer 170 – Abingdon, Wantage and Vale of the White Horse.
Landranger 175 – Reading and Windsor, Henley-on-Thames and Bracknell.

Transport: Rail – Tilehurst to Goring.
National Rail Enquiries – Tel: 0845 7484950.
Bus – Ridgeway Explorer, Miller of Mansfield PH, for timetable details, see Day 12.

Taxis: Goring-on-Thames
        • Apple Cars – Tel: 01491 874401.
        • Murdocks cars – Tel: 01491 872029.

Car Parking: Tilehurst railway station car park, or in one of the roads on the hill opposite.
Moulsford car park – in centre of village, next to telephone box.

Accommodation/Public Houses/Refreshments:
    Whitchurch-on-Thames
        • Ferry Boat Inn – Tel: 0118 9842161.
        • Greyhound Inn – Tel: 0118 9842160.
        • The Rectory, B&B – Tel: 0118 9843219.
    Goring-on-Thames
        • Riverside Tearooms – Tel: 01491 872243.
        • Mrs Wiltshire, Leyland, B&B – Tel: 01491 872119.
        • Mrs Ewen, 14 Mountfield B&B – Tel: 01491 872029.

- John Barleycorn PH, B&B – Tel: 01491 872509.
- Miller of Mansfield PH, B&B – Tel: 01491 872829.
- Queens Arms PH, B&B – Tel: 01491 872825.

Streatley
- Youth Hostel – Tel: 01491 872278.
- Swan Diplomat Hotel – Tel: 01491 878800.

Moulsford
- The Old Bakery Tearooms – Tel: 01491 651589.
- White House, B&B – Tel: 01491 651397.
- 22 Underhill, B&B – Tel: 01491 652133.
- Beetle and Wedge Hotel – Tel: 01491 651376.

For other travel and accommodation details, apply for the Ridgeway National Trail Companion – Tel: 01865 810224.

The place name Tilehurst is derived from the Old English *tigel* meaning tile, and *hurst*, a wooded hill; hence Tilehurst, a wooded hill where tiles are made. Potteries were operating here until the 1950s, there is an estate called 'The Potteries'. Some of these tiles can be seen at Whitchurch later on today's route. Retrace your steps on Day 12 from Tilehurst railway station back to the Roebuck Hotel to continue walking north-west on the right-hand side of the busy A329 road.

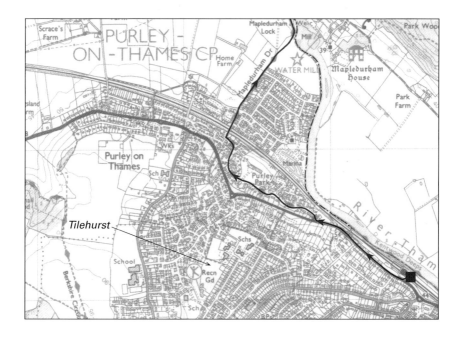

Pill-box, Tilehurst

Thirty yards from the Roebuck Hotel, there is a large, square, concrete block, a 'pill-box', a reminder of World War II. A series of these pill-boxes or defence positions were built to defend the River Thames in the event of a German invasion inland (see also Day 17).

Walk beside the road until just before Roebuck Rise on the left, then turn sharp right down some steps on the route of the Thames Path. Turn left into Skerritt Way, along Hazel Road, then right to cross the railway bridge. This bridge has two arches, the narrower of the two was used to take the Wilts/Berks canal before the canal was filled in. At the bottom of the hill, leave the road as it curves right, to bear left and follow the green acorn waymark. Turn right down Mapledurham Drive on the footpath. Where the gravelly footpath bears left, go through the kissing gate, across the water-meadow to the river. Here is Mapledurham Lock, where a notice explains that Mapledurham House (the large house partly hidden in the trees on the opposite bank), or otherwise Hardwick Hall (the gabled brick mansion visible further upstream on the far bank), could have provided Kenneth Grahame with his model for Toad Hall in his novel *The Wind in the Willows*. Continue to walk upstream on the bank of the River Thames, which still forms the county boundary between Berkshire on the far bank and Oxfordshire on the near bank, and into **Pangbourne** meadow. We saw turquoise damsel flies on the surface of the water in June.

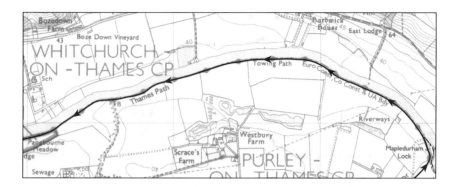

Access Point: Whitchurch-on-Thames car park, 4.25 miles. Pub, telephone at Whitchurch. Pangbourne Shops, post office, telephone, railway station, and public toilets in the car park (300 yards left (W) from route). GR 636768.

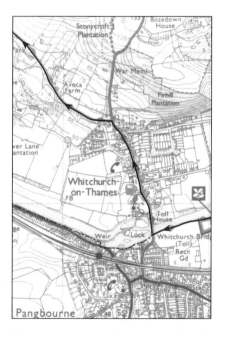

At **Whitchurch** bridge, bear away from the river and into a car park on the edge of Pangbourne. Leave the car park by climbing up the bank to the road. (There are toilets in a second car park a few yards further left along the road towards Pangbourne.) Turn right, and across this Victorian tollbridge with its toll-house. It is one of only two remaining tollbridges on the river Thames. Cross into Oxfordshire. Turn left on the far side along a drive signed 'The Mill and Church Cottages'. It is possible to identify the medieval bricks of the original mill to the left of the building, as they look duller in colour; the large Victorian extension is of brighter brick with the local Tilehurst tiles hung at the gables. There are also fine-gauged bricks over the arches of the window. Turn right in front of the mill, onto a narrow path leading up to the church.

Whitchurch is likely to be named after the pale stone church here although most of the church has been rebuilt in 14th century style. However, there is a fine exterior Norman door in the riverside wall of the church. Turn right out of the churchyard onto a private road. Turn left (N) at the main road and walk uphill through the village. There are several houses with tile-hung walls

Walk up the steep hill out of the village to the de-restriction sign, to turn left (W) following the white acorn waymark and Longacre Farm signs onto a tree-lined unmetalled road. As we walked in October we saw inkcap fungi, wild marjoram and bryony bordering the road here. The lane turns left, but continue straight ahead down the wooden steps. Here we have our first glimpse (look to the right) of one of the dry valleys leading down to the Goring Gap.

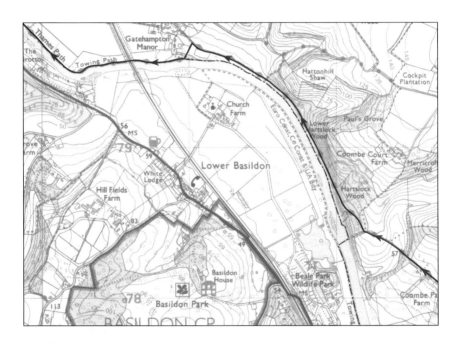

The Goring Gap
The Goring Gap was formed by meltwater from an ice sheet. In the Ice Age the Thames burst through the Chiltern Hills and so altered its course from its original one to London via St Albans. For thousands of years huge volumes of water wore away the soft chalk. Now the Goring Gap marks the change from the wide, flat, Thames Valley plain upstream to the steeper-sided valley at Goring. The distance between the hills is only 0.5 miles. The valley stretching up the meadow to the north east is likely to be a glacial dry valley, having been scraped out by the glacial moraine.

After climbing up the other side of the valley, the path enters an ancient wood, Hartslock Wood. There is butcher's broom growing here. This is a very primitive plant, which has red berries in October and is supposed to have been used by butchers. There are also spindle, yew trees, and wild privet with its black berries, smaller than those of the deadly nightshade, but just as poisonous.

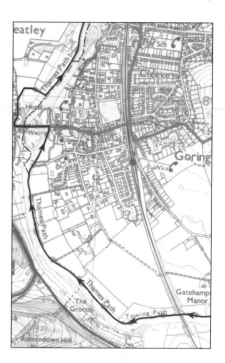

Walk on, high up on the chalky river cliff. There is another pill-box at the base of the cliff, which would have formerly guarded the river. Leave the wood on the path leading straight ahead, walking out of the gorge into the open country where the chalk cliffs are now 0.25 miles away from the river. After passing a paddock, turn left towards the river along a permitted right of way and past a buckthorn bush, also with poisonous black berries. On reaching the river, turn right, passing Gatehampton Manor to the right. These wide, flat banks provided a watering place for animals, such as reindeer and wild horse, in the Palaeolithic period. At Gatehampton Farm, stone tools have been found showing that this may have been where these animals were ambushed by primitive man taking advantage of the herds of animals. These tools are among the earliest found in Oxfordshire.

Walk along the riverside path under the splendid Gatehampton rail bridge, built by the famous engineer Brunel in 1840 and doubled in width in 1893. There is another pill-box tucked just beyond it.

We saw coot in among the bulrushes and grebe out in the river, and along the tree covered path we spotted a Small-leafed Lime tree.

Brunel bridge and pill-box, Gatehampton

The Small-leafed Lime (*Tilia cordata*).
GR 596804 (One hundred yards past the third small wooden bridge in front of the boat houses, in the trees to the right of the path, approaching Goring from the south). This tree is now very rare, even though common, seven thousand years ago. This species is a direct link with the primeval 'wild wood'. The reason for its scarcity is that it is an indicator of good soil and was therefore worth grubbing out to cultivate the land. It also suffers badly from browsing animals such as deer. Now that deer are 'running wild' rather than being kept in deer enclosures or deer parks, the small leaved lime has suffered. It looks superficially like a beech tree with a smooth bark, but has distinct heart-shaped broad leaves with long narrow tips. This particular specimen is growing with common limes whose leaves are bigger.

Small leaved lime and common lime

The banks of the river here have been sandbagged and piled to reduce erosion. Enter the village of **Goring** by the mill and its millrace.

Access Point: Goring-on-Thames, 8.8 miles. Car park and public toilets in village 500 yards east of route. Shops, post office, pubs, cafés, telephone, and railway station. GR 600807.

It is worth diverting to Goring church, which is a Norman priory church of flint and clunch (chalk), with sparing use of the more expensive yellow Taynton stone (see day 20).

At the Goring bridge, our path goes first right (E) up to the road where there is a café. Then turn left to cross the bridge into **Streatley** and **Berkshire**. There is a pale-blue and white college barge moored on the Berkshire bank. Walk past the Swan Hotel.

Access Point: Streatley, 9 miles. Pub, telephone, youth hostel. GR 594808.

An Ancient Crossing of the Thames
Between Streatley to the west and
Goring to the east, the river is broad
and shallow, and split into three
channels by islands. Crossing was
therefore made easy, and a notice-
board explains that Goring bridge,
which has replaced the ferry, is near
perhaps the oldest crossing-place of
the Thames: a ford at the end of
Ferry Lane in Goring (GR 595604).
It was used in prehistoric times
when the Ridgeway and Icknield Way
provided a trade route from Dorset
to East Anglia. The ford continued
to be important to the Romans who
built a raised causeway. Villages
grew up by the crossing and in
Anglo-Saxon times the river formed
a frontier: Streatley in Wessex and
Goring in Mercia. Streatley was
originally the larger of the two
villages, and remained so while the
coaching route to Oxford passed
through it. When the railway was
built on the opposite bank in
Goring, it attracted more of the
trade and so grew larger than
Streatley.

Further up the street on the left, is another chamfered corner on 1, Icknield Cottages (see Days 5 and 11). Turn right (N) to follow the Thames Path past Streatley church. Keep right where the paths divide and follow the sign 'To the river'. This green lane is causewayed and was used to keep the travellers' feet dry above the flood water. It is studded with ancient standard ash trees and is likely to be the original path to a ferry in a pre-bridge age. The remains of the stone causeway can be seen leading to the river bank. Turn left upstream past some elegantly painted boathouses on the far bank, and over a footbridge This crosses the entrance to a winding pool where narrow-boats can be turned.

At the end of the water-meadow, pass Cleeve Lock where there is a flood level plaque on the right of the lock-keeper's cottage. To the west, there are views of the Berkshire Downs. Keep to the river bank through the water-meadows. Just north of some trees at Runsford Hole, the county boundary leaves the river and goes southwest along the hedgeline. We leave Berkshire here, enter Oxfordshire and shall be following its new direction on Day 14.

Pass the riverside houses of **Moulsford**, to the front of the Beetle and Wedge Hotel. Turn left by this historic inn. As the inn sign indicates, the name of the hotel originates from the mallet and wedge used in wood splitting. This was also the inn where H. G. Wells worked on the novel *The History of Mr Polly*. Go up the lane, and though our route goes left for Day 14, turn right onto the main road (A329) for car parking. Walk north on the **Moulsford** village street for 500 yards to the centre of the village. The car park is on the left where there is a telephone and restaurant/teashop.

Day Fourteen

MOULSFORD TO WEST ILSLEY

Moulsford GR 590839 to West Ilsley GR 470826

This day on top of the Berkshire Downs provides wide skyscapes. Farmers have successfully farmed rabbits, sheep and arable crops here, but these wide, open, unfenced stretches are also ideal for the horse-racing world. We reach 150 miles along our way on the top of Hodcott Down, and end the day in the shelter of one of the isolated villages which provided food and water to both animal and man.

Distance: 10.2 miles (16 km).

Maps: Explorer 170 – Abingdon, Wantage & Vale of White Horse.
Landranger 174 – Newbury, Wantage & surrounding area.

Transport: Ridgeway Explorer: Bus stops – East Ilsley, Broad Street, and West Ilsley, The Harrow PH. (For details, see Day 12)

Taxis: Compton   • Compton Passenger Service – Tel: 01635 579076.
Blewbury   • Rural Connections – Tel: 01235 851010.
Didcot   • Bob's – Tel: 01235 512121/814679.
     • Pryor's – Tel: 01235 812345.
Wantage   • Grove Taxis – Tel: 01235 770000.
     • Keith's Cabs – Tel: 01235 763344.

Car Parking: Moulsford – at the north end of the village.
West Ilsley – limited parking either by the duck-pond, or in the village street, near the church.

Accommodation/Public Houses/Refreshments:
None on route.
Nearest B&Bs are:
East Ilsley (1.3 miles from route)
       • Swan Hotel, B&B – Tel: 01635 281238.
       • Kennett House, B&B. Mr & Mrs C Grieve –
         Tel: 01635 281364/281778.

Compton (1.5 miles from route)
  - Compton Swan Hotel – Tel: 01635 578765.
West Ilsley - The Harrow PH (no B&B) – Tel: 01635 281260.
  Shop and P.O.

Several other B&Bs listed at villages of Blewbury, East Hendred and in the town of Wantage, all in the Ridgeway National Trail Companion – Tel: 01865 810224.

Vale and Downland Museum, Church Street, Wantage – Tel: 01235 771447, (with café).

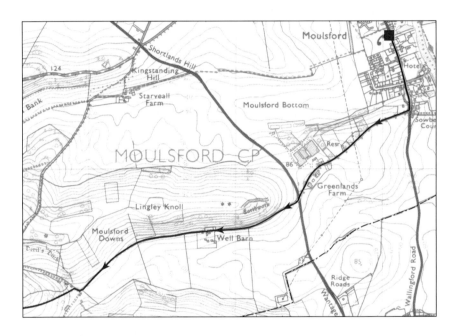

Turn right out of **Moulsford**'s car park and walk south beside the A329 road. The timber-framed brick cottages on the left are built 'gable-end' onto the road. Many older houses were built 'gable-end' for two possible reasons, to make them more secure than if their front doors faced onto the road, or to make use of the narrow plots.

Where Ferry Lane joins the road from the Beetle and Wedge Hotel, cross to the right side of the road. Take great care as it is busy and there is no footpath. The road is an ancient sunken way with steep chalk sides. At the 'Slow' sign near the crest of the hill, turn right (W) up a steep chalk-sided byway which was probably a former chalk pit. Walk up the track with its large multi-specied hedges. The present county boundary is one field to the left, but until 1972 it was along the River Thames all the way to Buscot, several miles upstream from Oxford.

Gable-end houses, Moulsford

  Pass Greenlands Farm and cross the A417 road. Continue up to the Well Farm Estate. In November, we saw scabious, deadnettle and yarrow out in flower here. On approaching Well Barn Farm, look left across the valley, where a section of scrubby vegetation partially covers the remains of the ancient cultivation along the contour lines (lynchets as in Day 3). In other places, the modern ploughing has eliminated all signs. The place name 'Well Barn' is interesting, as it is one of the few places where someone has sunk a well into the chalk.

  Continue on the metalled lane, past buckthorn and spindle bushes (the latter having bright, rose-pink fruits in winter), to a small wooden cottage. Then bear right (NW) to a wooden pavilion, and left and upwards to follow a waymarked footpath, signed 'Keepers Cottage 1.5 miles'. To the left, there is hazel coppicing in the woodland. Near the top of the stony track, where a footpath joins from the right, there is a grassy gap in the woodland to the left. A wide 'ride' is visible in the woodland opposite, with a solitary fir tree in the middle of it (GR 556817).

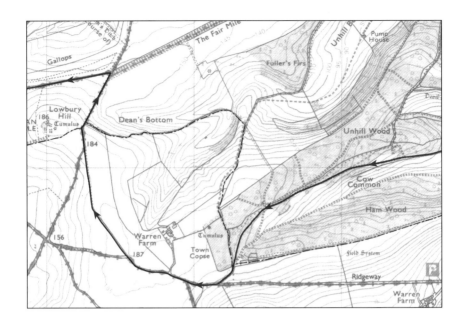

Pheasant shooting

This area is used for shooting, particularly pheasants. The beaters flush out the birds which fly across the ride, and the sportsman shoots at them as they cross. This is a similar method to that used in deer hunting in medieval times: hence place names, such as Kingstanding Hill to the north east (GR 574836).

Rabbit farming

We are also walking through country which was used for breeding rabbits in the late 18th and early 19th centuries, as indicated by Warren Farm to the south (GR 566811), Warren Farm to the west (GR 548816), and Streatley Warren (GR 555809). It was very difficult to make a living up here during most of the 19th century, so the farmers diversified and encouraged the introduction of rabbit-warrens. The rabbits were bred for the London food and fur markets.

Follow a fine woodland bank on the right. At the junction of the tracks at GR 555817 continue straight on through the woods on the waymarked path. Bear left (SW) on the path, passing right of a keeper's cottage on the edge of the wood, then go over a stile to cross the county boundary into **Berkshire**. Our path enters open ground. Go downhill, and bear right to join the Ridgeway. Looking up to the left slope opposite, there are good examples of the remains of a Romano-British field system. There are signs of the raised banks bounding the small, square fields. Keep travelling west. The landscape has changed to open downland but the track is, for the time being, between multi-specied hedges with sloe trees. Where a byway enters from the left (SE), keep straight ahead in a west-north-west direction on the Ridgeway. There are splendid views to the left (S) across the Berkshire Downs. Five hundred yards from where the byway joined, the Ridgeway branches left (W), but we bear right onto a footpath alongside a former hedgerow. Here are orange-coloured sarsen stones cleared to the field edges by farmers. There are views of Wittenham Clumps to the right. We cross back into **Oxfordshire** just before Lowbury Hill. The skyscapes are wonderful. In November we saw large flocks of migrating birds, and on January 2nd skylarks were aloft, heralding the new year on a fine, cold but sunny day.

Lowbury Hill
Lowbury Hill, an ancient ritual site with a Romano-British shrine on its top, has long continued to be important, as the presence of Anglo-Saxon tumuli indicate. The field in which the Roman temple was sited is private land now, but standing near this lofty setting it is easy to imagine the Romans worshipping their gods, Mercury and Mars. On a more earthly level, oyster shell remains can be found: a reminder that Romans ate oysters. To the north-west, the buildings of the Harwell International Business Centre (formerly AERE Harwell) can be seen (see Day 15). Didcot power station is visible ahead (N).

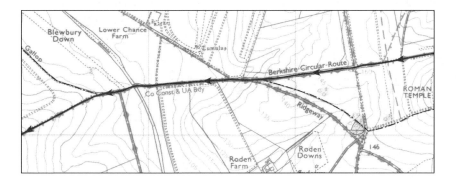

From Lowbury Hill, bear right (NE) down a steep, stony track between ancient hedgerows to a crossing of two tracks where the land flattens. One is the Fair Mile to the east, which is a wide path typical of the ancient Ridgeway. Turn sharp left here and continue (W) beside the racehorse gallops. The Ridgeway joins the track after 1 mile, and we now walk on the county boundary for 0.6 miles, passing over the bridge above the dismantled Didcot/Newbury/Southampton railway. There are several fir coppices to the left.

0.4 miles to our right, and east of the former railway, is Lower Chance Farm (GR 520827). This brick building was the armoury of a tented military camp set up in summer for training Volunteer (later Territorial) regiments. There was live firing practice northwards to butts on Churn Hill. What remains of Churn Station, which serviced the camp, is 300 yards along the line from the bridge.

On descending towards **East Ilsley**, there is a series of tracks indicating a succession of use: as each track became too muddy, another was made. Continue ahead uphill for another 0.7 miles to a concrete track, passing the Ridgeway National Trail notice of 'The Code of Respect'. Turn right (NW) along this track.

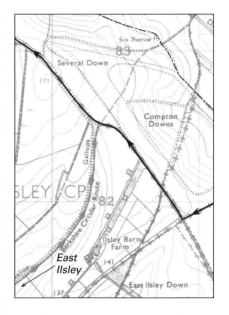

Sheep rearing

The grassy track ahead is one of several drove roads converging towards the village of **East Ilsley** which was once one of the biggest sheep markets in the area. It was situated in the centre of the sheep-rearing area where, it is said, that up to 80,000 sheep could change hands within a few days. This village is now famous for its race horse stables and our path passes some of the gallops.

Access Point: For nearer access continue straight ahead at this point to join the road (1.3 mile diversion) into East Ilsley, 8.2 miles. Pub, telephone. GR 493812.

Five hundred yards from the sharp-right turn, there is a water tap by the end of the wood (GR 506823), dedicated to Dr D. Phillip, general practitioner in the Newbury district (1945–1974). Pass another byway leading to East Ilsley. The noise of the A34 increases as Several Down (Old English for 'privately enclosed') is climbed. Here the county boundary runs roughly parallel to the Ridgeway near the bottom of the slope to the right (NE). It also forms the local parish boundaries. On the right side of the track, 200 yards east of the A34, is a stone memorial to Hugh Frederick Grosvenor aged 19 years, a second-lieutenant of the Lifeguards who lost his life in an armoured-car accident while on military duty on April 9th 1947.

Continue on the main path, passing a small wood to the right, and go into a tunnel. Decorating the left side of the tunnel are murals depicting the history of the villages of Compton Hundred. These illustrate first the Beaker Folk; the Battle of Ashdown in 871 AD, when Alfred defeated the Danes; the East Ilsley sheep fair and the Royal Charter. On the other side of the tunnel, native species have been planted: small, round, black berries we identified as wild privet; the glossy scarlet berries confirmed guelder rose; the red stalks, dogwood; and the oval, black seeds, a way-faring tree.

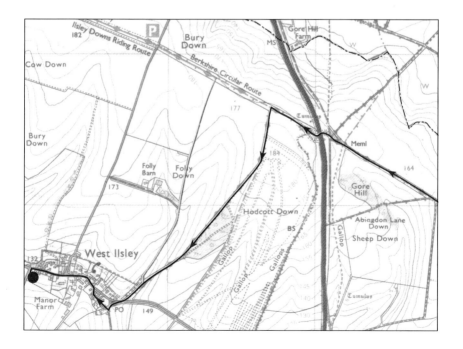

The Ridgeway

At the top of the slope, the Ridgeway (which varies in width along its route) opens out into a broad zone of communication, without hedgerows or fence lines. In the days of the East Ilsley fairs, this was ideal for moving large numbers of sheep. The Vale and Downland museum in Wantage (see above) includes a lively presentation of the history of the Ridgeway.

The Ridgeway, north east of West Ilsley

Ignore the first path leaving left at the top of the tunnel exit slope, and continue on the Ridgeway for 200 yards to where a second path leaves left. Turn onto it, and after 400 yards, bear right onto the track. Here, on top of Hodcott Down (GR 486833) marks 150 miles around our boundary walk. The track leads off the Downs to **West Ilsley** village. On joining the road at the chapel, turn right past the Post Office and shop, and walk towards the church, where flints have been used due to a lack of other local building stone. Continue to the duck-pond, which is ornamental now, but (along with other similar ponds in Compton and East Ilsley) provided important staging sites when the Ridgeway was used for the movement of livestock in the south of England. The Harrow public house nearby provides modern refreshment for humans!

Duck pond, West Ilsley

Day Fifteen

WEST ILSLEY TO FAWLEY

West Ilsley GR470826 to Fawley GR392813

A day spent, at first high up on the Berkshire Downs escarpment with wide views across the Vale of White Horse, then into the dry chalky stretches of land on the dip slope. We pass isolated houses such as Lands End, and the village of Farnborough, with its gem of a church window, to reach Fawley in its high, lonely position which Thomas Hardy chose as a setting for his bleakest novel, Jude the Obscure.

Distance: 12 miles (19.1 km).

Maps: Explorer 170 – Abingdon, Wantage and Vale of White Horse.
Landranger 174 – Newbury, Wantage and surrounding area.

Transport: Ridgeway Explorer bus stops (see Day 12 for details) at West Ilsley, Farnborough Church and Court Hill Road, near YHA Ridgeway Centre (see below).

Taxis: Didcot
Wantage

- Bob's – Tel: 01235 512121. Mobile 0860 265158.
- Keith's Cabs – Tel: 01235 763346
- Sapphire Cars – Tel: 01235 772424.
- Supercab Taxis – Tel: 01235 770000.

Car Parking: West Ilsley – limited parking either by the duck-pond, or in the village street near the church.
Fawley – on the village green.

Accommodation/Public Houses/Refreshments:

East Hendred
- Ridgeway Lodge Hotel – Tel: 01235 833360. GR 460873 1.5 miles from route.

Farnborough
- The Old Smithy – Tel: 01488 638782. Mobile 04020 95371.

Lockinge
- Kiln Farm – Tel: 01635 763308. GR 423833 1.1 miles from route.

132

Letcombe Regis • YHA Ridgeway Centre – Tel: 01235 768865.
GR 393849 1.3 miles from route.

Wantage 3.1 miles from route: Tourist Information Centre – Tel: 01235 760176 for
other accommodation or at Letcombe Regis 2.4 miles from route.

Retrace your steps from either the duck-pond or near the church in **West Ilsley** (see Day 14) by walking (SE) along the village street towards East Ilsley. Many of the houses and farm buildings have half-hipped roofs. This economical design allowed shorter and therefore cheaper timbers to be used for the main rafters. Pass the little chapel on the right, and go as far as the de-restriction sign at the end of the village. Turn left (NE) uphill at the 'cart-track' sign. Just after a row of houses, the track divides. Take the left (W) fork, to walk uphill and past the bridleway sign (left to Folly Barn), and continue up the dip slope of the Berkshire Downs to the Ridgeway at the top. Turn left (W) and walk along the Ridgeway, and across the minor road.

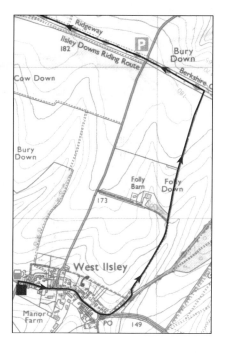

Access Point: Bury Down car park, 1.8 miles. GR 479840.

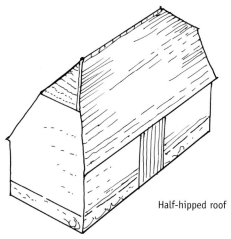

Half-hipped roof

Grims Ditch

On looking north from the Ridgeway and down the slope, a line of trees, a ditch and an embankment can be seen. This is the Pre Roman Iron Age Grims Ditch which lies 500 yards below the crest, where it runs parallel with the Ridgeway for about twelve miles. This linear earthwork, attributed to the devil, *Grim*, demarcated an area of 'ranching' on the Downs from the arable fields in the Vale. It was a territorial rather than a military boundary. The county boundary follows the irregular route of Grims Ditch along the bottom of the hill.

The Tale of DIDO, PLUTO, GLEEP, BEPO, and LIDO

At the base of the slope to our right, are two cylindrical steel buildings, looking rather like big, shiny dustbins. They housed nuclear reactors, one called DIDO (so named because it used 'heavy water' or deuterium oxide – D_2O), and the other PLUTO (its name continuing a tradition of using mythical names ending in an 'O'), which were built in the AERE Harwell complex to help scientists design Britain's nuclear power stations. Harwell's first reactor – GLEEP (Graphite Low Energy Experimental Pile) was constructed in 1947, and operated without incident for 43 years. BEPO (British Experimental Pile) was the second reactor to be built, and LIDO was a reactor that looked like a swimming pool, with blue, glowing, fuel rods under twenty feet of water. Only DIDO and PLUTO remain. It will take until 2040 before their radioactivity has decayed sufficiently for them to be demolished. The whole site is historically famous, as it was from RAF Harwell that British troops took off to be the first to land in Normandy on D-Day, 5th June 1945. Today, Harwell International Business Centre is home to over thirty high-tech companies. The wind turbines seen to the west are experimental electricity generators belonging to the Rutherford-Appleton Laboratory.

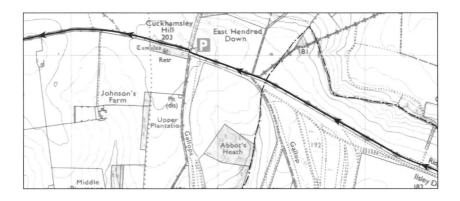

There are gallops to the left of the Ridgeway; race horse training is a major industry on the Downs. Just before the confluence of three other paths (GR 463849), we cross the county boundary into Oxfordshire, its route now following the course of the parish boundaries (see Days 16 and 17). Another 550 yards along the track, there is a clump of pine trees and a tarmac road up to the Ridgeway path. Continue straight ahead along the Ridgeway in a westerly direction. In wet weather, it is worth taking the path through the wood by **Scutchamer Knob**.

Access Point: Scutchamer Knob car park, 3.2 miles. GR 458851.

Scutchamer Knob
This mound to the south of the Ridgeway is thought to have been a Saxon royal barrow (marked tumulus on the map) which hides the remains of, or commemorates, Cwichelm, a pagan Anglo-Saxon king who lived in the early 7th century. This barrow is very much bigger than the Bronze Age barrows or tumuli scattered over the Downs. It has been ruthlessly robbed, so that now it is hardly the conical hill that it originally was. This mound marked one of the 'hundred' meeting places of Berkshire representatives. A 'hundred' was an administrative area of Anglo-Saxon England.

Zones of Communication Overhead
A modern daily reminder of the time is once again the sight and sound of *Concorde* at 11am on weekdays and 10.30am on Sundays. The Berkshire Downs are situated under the airway 'Green One' which refers to a series of radio navigation beacons; one on the former Hampstead Norreys airfield; the next westwards on the Brecon Beacons; the next one at Merthyr Tydfil; then further westwards to Fishguard and finally to New York. Hence *Concorde's* predictable passage overhead each day.

Walk on past a fir copse, ignoring the footpath sign to the left. Just beyond the copse at GR 443850, it is possible to go through the metal farm gate on the north side of the Ridgeway to find, behind a small tree, a large sarsen stone engraved: 'In memory of Penelope Betjeman (1910–1986), the poet John Betjeman's wife, who loved the Ridgeway'. The Betjemans lived in the village of Lockinge in the valley below and Penelope Betjeman used to enjoy riding on the Downs.

Retrace your steps, to continue west along the Ridgeway for another 0.7 miles. At GR 433846, at a sign 'The Ridgeway', there is a track joining the Ridgeway from the left (SE). Turn back along this track, to walk beside the barbed-wire fence towards a wooded area. This is Wether Down (*wether* = young male sheep). This is a dry valley.

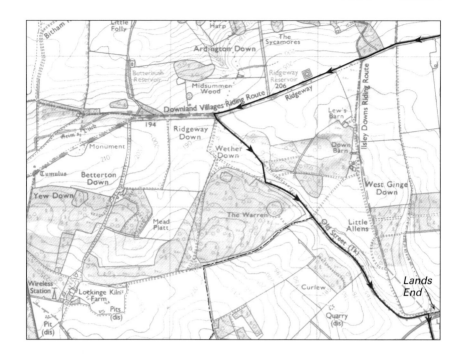

Farming on the Downs

This part of the Downs has been under cultivation at irregular intervals. Two hundred years ago during the Napoleonic wars, these agricultural fluctuations were caused by the operation of 'the continental system' whereby France, which was in control of Europe from 1802–1815, prevented the export of corn to Britain. This encouraged British farmers to plough up every available acre to produce home-grown corn. At the end of the war, foreign competition caused a disastrous slump in home produced corn prices, which meant that the Berkshire Downs again reverted to sheep runs. During the World Wars of the 20th century there was more ploughing and cultivation of these thin chalk soils. Since 1950, with the introduction of heavy mechanised farming and chemical fertilisers, it has been possible to put the Downs to continuous arable cultivation. This has, however, had a disastrous effect on the archaeological monuments, such as ancient field systems and tumuli.

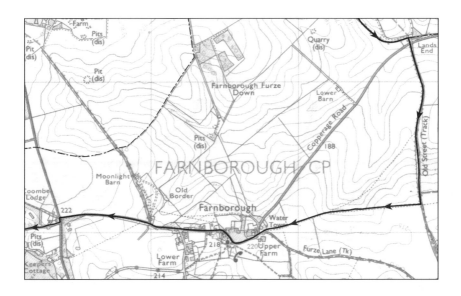

The wood to your right is called The Warren, another reminder that this was an area of rabbit breeding (see Day 14).

After leaving the woods, we reach the county boundary where two tracks cross. Continue ahead walking down the base of the valley along the route of the county boundary, with Berkshire to the right and Oxfordshire to the left. After 0.7 miles on this track called 'Old Street', Lands End Cottage is reached. Cross the road to continue uphill on Old Street, which is now a green lane and a footpath, though remains of ancient paving can be seen on the roadside opposite the cottage. Climb steeply, then just past a bridleway sign on the left , continue on ahead for another 80 yards, as far as the public footpath sign hidden in the hedge, and turn right (W) near the top of the hill. This footpath is further uphill than is marked on the map, so the compass bearing now actually reads 264° instead of the 275° on the map. Go west across the field to the gate on the far side, then along the footpath on the left of the hedge towards the farm buildings of **Farnborough** village. On arriving at the road, opposite Home Farm, turn left to walk in front of the gardens and 'ha-ha' (ditch) of The Old Rectory where John Betjeman (1906–1984) and his wife lived for some time. The rectory is built partly of grey vitrified bricks and is early Georgian with finials (c1749). There is a splendid vista here across the Downs.

'Ha-ha', Farnborough Old Rectory — *view blocked by hedge and fence*

'Ha-ha', Farnborough Old Rectory — *unrestricted view by digging a ditch*

Walk on west along the narrow road with great care. A visit to All Saints Church is recommended, as it is graced by a brilliant, modern, stained-glass window called 'The Tree of Life', a memorial to Sir John Betjeman, designed by his friend John Piper.

In the churchyard, there are the base and stump of a medieval preaching cross and an ancient sundial. On three sides of the church tower, just below the battlements, are the carvings of grotesque heads of beasts used as gargoyles.

Access Point: Farnborough, 7.9 miles. Car parking is very limited. Telephone. GR 436819.

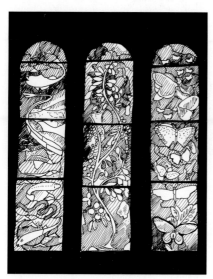

John Piper window, Farnborough

Continue west along the village street. At a wrought-iron road-junction sign by the Old Smithy, continue on in the direction of Wantage along the road and beyond the village for 0.6 miles. At the next junction at GR 424821, turn left past some brick cottages, then immediately right along the bridleway. Continue west beside the southern edge of the wood on a grassy track. Join a stony cart-track and turn left (SW) along it, beside a young beech wood. Take the first right turn (NW) onto a bridleway passing Little Coombe Farm to the right. We were lucky to see a covey of grey partridge as we walked here in December. Keep along the track on the right side of Sparrow's Copse.

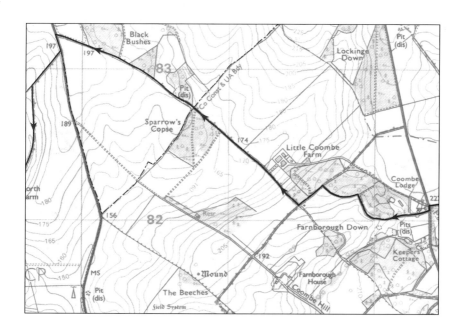

Traditional Woodland Management System

This woodland is a good example of ancient 'coppice and standards', a common practice in central and southern England. Coppicing involved hazel being cut down to the ground; seven years later poles were harvested from the young shoots. These poles were used for fencing, hurdles, wattle and thatching. 'Standards' are large single trees, usually oak, beech, elm or ash, left to grow into timber. This provided material for building houses, ships etc.

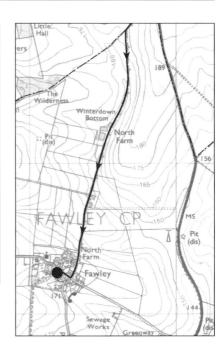

There are sarsen stones along the edge of this woodland which have been cleared from the field. There is a prominent woodland bank. At the far (N) edge of the wood, we re-enter Oxfordshire where the county boundary crosses our path. A hedge follows its course on the right (E) side, and the boundary demarcates the western edge of Sparrow's Copse to the left. Hazel catkins were growing in the wood in December, which was full of birds, including a large flock of long-tailed tits. Continue (NW) passing the woods called 'Black Bushes' to reach the busy A338 Wantage/Hungerford road. Turn left (S), taking care on crossing the road, and after 100 yards, bear right (SW) down a bridleway. This hedged path is the county boundary. Walk for 250 yards to a sharp bend, then bear left down the track to the hollow of Winterdown Bottom. This was chosen by Thomas Hardy as the site of Farmer Troutham's field in the vivid opening of *Jude the Obscure*. Jude, the young orphan, is sent to a 'wide and lonely depression in the general level of the upland, which was sown as a corn-field'. Here his task was to scare off the rooks. Our path continues through Fawley Stud towards the village of **Fawley**. Turn right at the village road, past the post office to the village green.

Day Sixteen

FAWLEY TO
ASHDOWN HOUSE

Fawley GR 392813 to Ashdown House GR 284823

Still on the sparsely populated chalky uplands — there are no villages, no public telephones, let alone beer(!) as we travel westwards. We criss-cross the boundary and learn the reason for its somewhat surprising route midway along the dip slope. We pass a remarkable group of Neolithic burial places and end the day to be greeted by the delightful elegance of Ashdown House.

Distance: 12.3 miles (18 km).

Maps: Explorer 170 – Abingdon, Wantage and Vale of White Horse.
Landranger 174 – Newbury, Wantage and surrounding area.

Transport: Ridgeway Explorer – Tel: 01793 522243. Bus stops at Sparsholt Firs, GR 343851, 0.3 miles from route, and at the Rose and Crown Hotel, Ashbury, GR 265851.

Taxis: Wantage   • Keith's Cabs – Tel: 01235 763346
                            • Sapphire Cars – Tel: 01235 772424.
                            • Supercab Taxis – Tel: 01235 770000.
            Lambourn   • Pottinger's Car & Minibus Services – Tel: 01488 72185.
                            • Ray's Taxis – Tel: 01488 71819.
            Shrivenham   • Briant's Hire – Tel: 01793 782206.

Car Parking: Fawley – on the village green.
Ashdown House – in the National Trust car park.

Accommodation/Public Houses/Refreshments:

            Sparsholt Down   • Mrs Reid, Down Barn Farm – Tel: 01367 820272.
                                GR 334852, 1.8 miles from route.

Ashbury 2.25 miles from Ashdown House
- Rose and Crown Hotel – Tel: 01793 710222.
  Car shuttle service to and from Ashdown House
  may be available.
- The Village Stores, B&B – Tel: 01793 710262.

Ridgeway Companion for comprehensive list – Tel: 01865 10224.
www.nationaltrails.gov.uk.

Newbury Tourist Information Centre – Tel: 01635 30267.

From the village green, walk west out of **Fawley** on the road towards the Downs (i.e. away from the A338 road).

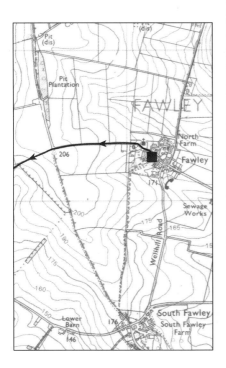

Fawley and *Jude the Obscure*
Fawley church is described in Thomas Hardy's novel *Jude the Obscure* as, 'a tall new building of modern Gothic design, unfamiliar to English eyes, (which) had been erected by a certain obliterator of historic records who had run down from London and back in a day'. You also pass the thatched cottage on the left with its small window panes (which is thought to have been possibly the model for Aunt Druscilla's), and the school where Hardy's orphaned grandmother suffered. It is her name, Mary, that Hardy gives to Marygreen as the pseudonym for Fawley, and the recollection of her unhappy memories is the reason for setting the book in this part of the country which was formerly Wessex. The school was where the character Mr Phillotson taught, and the rookery in the trees to the left was home to the rooks that Jude was sent to scare in Farmer Troutham's field (see Day 15).

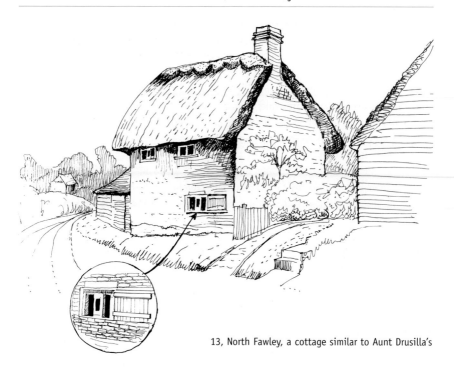

13, North Fawley, a cottage similar to Aunt Drusilla's

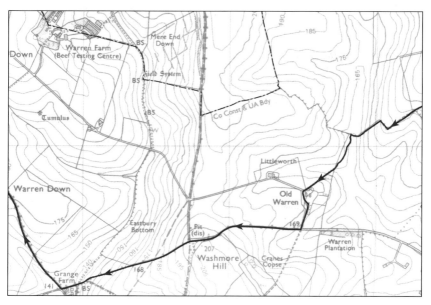

Where the road turns right (N), go straight ahead, walking west along the footpath past the trigonometrical point on the left. Walking here on the top of the Downs in January, we saw hares chasing each other. Follow the ancient, multi-specied hedge that sits on top of a lynchet. Climb the stile at the field boundary, and walk around the northern and western perimeter of the field. There are fine beech trees in the thick hedge. We saw fieldfares and yellowhammers here and a herd of fallow deer. Before taking the path along the right side of the wood, we recommend that you look back across the field to see the top of the Jacobean manor house with its embattled towers at South Fawley.

At Old Warren Farm (the name reminding us again of the tradition of rearing rabbits), bear left around the farm buildings. This farmhouse is timber-framed with brick in-filling as there was a shortage of stone for building material. Continue (S) along a concrete track and where the road turns left, turn right (W) along the bridleway, climbing up to Washmore Hill. We saw numerous flocks of field-fares and chaffinches feeding on the berries in the generous hedge on our right. At the 'crossroads' of the tracks, continue straight ahead (SW) down a hedged, sunken way towards Grange Farm (Grange = *Grangia* from the Latin meaning barn). Walk beyond where a track joins from the left (S), and past a barn, to the three wooden sheds in front of the house, then turn right (NW) along the byway climbing to Warren Down. Continue for 1.25 miles along this track towards the rust-red painted barn (known locally as the Red Barn). To the right (NE) is another Warren Farm on the county boundary, now a national centre for beef testing, hence the surprising number of cars passing the Red Barn in such an isolated situation. Nearby, to the left of the barn is Bockhampton Down, a piece of grassy downland with open access. We heard corn buntings and skylarks singing in March and saw a buzzard glide overhead. Bear right (NW) from the barn

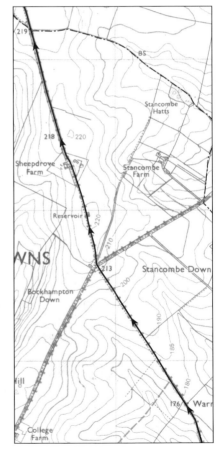

along an asphalted track signposted 'Sparsholt Firs'. Here, high on the Lambourn Downs, are superb views northwards to the Vale of White Horse and westwards towards the Marlborough Downs. Pass a reservoir to the right of the track. East Ditch, a prehistoric ranch boundary, is visible on the side of Wormhill Bottom to the left of Sheepdrove Farm.

This track is a good example of a drove road. It is wide (at least 30–40 feet across) and is home to yellow/green striped snails and wild flowers such as knapweed. The county boundary crosses our track on the brow of the hill where a thin hedgerow joins from the right (E), then goes north-west to the B4001 road from Wantage to Lambourn. There is no right of way along here, so our route continues (NW) towards Sparsholt Firs and the radio mast, and joins the road close to the Ridgeway there.

Access Point: Sparsholt Firs, 5.5 miles. GR 341845.

On joining the B4001, turn left (S), walking 0.75 miles beside it. Take care, it is busy and traffic travels fast! The rewards for the diversion north are the superb views to the west over the Marlborough Downs. In winter, on your right, you can see a

The History of the Berkshire/ Oxfordshire Boundaries

Some people may wonder why the county boundary between Oxfordshire to the north and Berkshire to the south does not follow the path of the Ridgeway. The county boundary used to follow the River Thames for over 40 miles, until the local government reform in 1972 when Oxfordshire was enlarged by the addition of a large piece of north-west Berkshire. The present county boundary was redrawn along the southern edge of the parish boundaries of the settlements which extend from the Vale of the White Horse and terminate in the chalk downs. This means that the new southern boundary of Oxfordshire runs along ancient parish and estate boundaries which go back at least a thousand years.

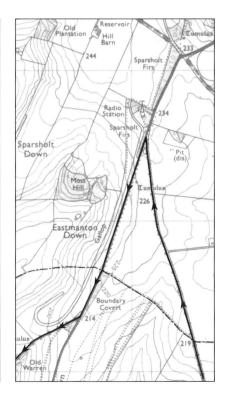

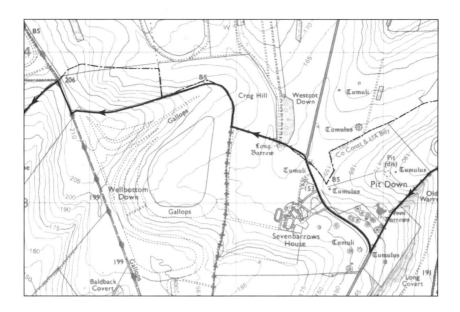

series of ploughed-out ancient fields which are below the shelter belt on the skyline of this slope. The ancient field boundaries show up as whitish and the soil between them is dark brown. This gives a network of light field boundaries and dark fields. Cross the county boundary, beyond which is the wood called Boundary Covert. Where this wood ends, pass the notice 'Valley of the Racehorse' and bear right (SW) to take a chalky byway.

Access Point: Bridleway entrance onto B4001, 6.3 miles. GR 336833.

Walk downhill beside a 'hanger' of beech trees and a series of gallops on the left. The track joins a minor road beside a remarkable monument. We are entering the land of tumuli. There is one with trees planted on it, high up on the slope to the right, and a further cluster at the bottom of the slope. This is the famous Seven Barrows group, which is dated to the Bronze Age.

Access Point: Seven Barrows, 6.9 miles. GR 329827.

At the road, turn sharp right (NW) and walk through the reserve, or along the road, then past Sevenbarrows House on the left. There are more barrows to the right. Marked on the map is 'BS' (boundary stone) but now the boundary to the right is indicated by an iron marker. Take the track left along the county boundary and through the gap in the wooden fence to keep to the footpath along the southern end of the wood.

The Seven Barrows Group

There are now seven obvious barrows to be seen, but originally there were forty-six. All the others have been ploughed-out or are single barrows way up on the Downs. This probably was a major ritual site in the Bronze Age (1800–500 BC). It is interesting that the network of small fields on the ridge to the north (the traces of which we saw as we walked along the road) does not extend down to this valley site. The valley appears to have been kept free of arable agriculture in the Bronze Age and the Pre-Roman Iron Age. Whether this was simply due to the ritual significance of the place or whether it was pastoral country is not apparent. A number of these barrows have been excavated: some of them are bowl barrows (with a shape like an inverted Christmas pudding basin), some disc barrows (like a saucer) and some bell barrows (shaped like a bell with a flange and a ditch outside the flange). The one nearest the path to your right is a disc barrow and it does look just like a saucer. It is very unusual to have a barrow group like this deep down in the bottom of a valley as, on the Downs, they are usually on the ridges and on the margins of cultivation. The Seven Barrows are a Scheduled Ancient Monument and the notice board indicates they are also a BBOWT Nature Reserve with permitted access via the paths as shown. The thirteen acres of ungrazed chalk grassland surrounding the archaeological site are a Site of Special Scientific Interest. The grassland has never been ploughed and over a hundred plant species have been recorded. The plant community provides the larval food for the rich butterfly population. It is one of only 266 hectares of the original, flower-rich, chalk grassland remaining in Oxfordshire.

The Seven Barrows, north of Upper Lambourn

Long Barrows
The long barrow marked on the map is here, at the edge of the wood; indeed the footpath crosses the mound of earth. This is the remains of the Lambourn Neolithic long barrow. It has been excavated and originally had several stone chambers. Within them were buried the disarticulated skeletal remains of a large number of people, probably all related. These people farmed this upland area of the Downs in about 3500–3000 BC. Such a communal barrow would have been for a family ruling over hundreds of years. Some of the other barrows of the Cotswold region are thought to have been used over a period of, perhaps, a thousand years.

Walk another 400 yards to where the bridleway, on the county boundary, turns right (N) and follow the boundary as it curves up and west on the hill beside the gallops. The series of numbered markers by the gallops indicate the furlong intervals that are still used in the horse racing world: there are eight furlongs to the mile. At the top of the hill, turn right (N) where we join the Lambourn Valley Way for 150 yards, then left (SW) down Whit Coombe (*Whit Combe* = white valley in old English) along the county boundary again.

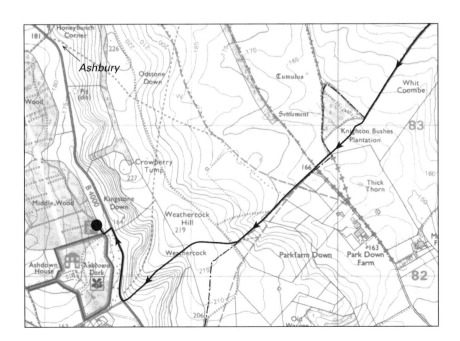

This may seem a featureless landscape but it was used for sheep farming in the Middle Ages, so one would not expect any remains of buildings or walls. Sheep, herded by a shepherd and dog, do not need permanent fencing. The shepherd would have carried his hurdles with him and folded the sheep at night with them. The lack of fences thus indicate the management patterns that were followed over hundreds of years, those of alternating sheep/corn husbandry.

At the bottom of the Coombe, the bridleway has been diverted from its original route across the field. Instead, turn right and follow the southern edge of Knighton Bushes Plantation, turn left (S) on meeting the farm track, then right (SW) at the junction of the tracks up towards Weathercock Hill. A wind-blasted tree on the top, can be seen if visibility is good. On looking right (N), there is a fine view of Uffington Castle, the Pre-Roman Iron Age fort on White Horse Hill. Pass the meeting of the footpaths in the bottom of the valley, and start up the steep part of the hill. A track leaves to the right (SW), but continue on up the steep slope, past huge sarsen stones along the county boundary (for explanation of sarsen stones see Day 10). Halfway up, there are remains of a prominent lynchet, which has been ploughed out, in the field beside the path. At the top of the hill, at another sarsen stone, go straight ahead (W 270°) across the field along the signed footpath, keeping the clump of hawthorn bushes to the left (S). Cross a stile, where the copper-roofed cupola and golden ball finial on the roof of Ashdown House and the weather vane of Weathercock Hill are visible. Ahead of us lies an interesting piece of historical landscape.

On this hillside you are free to take whichever path you wish. To take the direct route to the stile opposite the car park, walk west (292°), between the weather vane and the wind-blasted tree, but be warned, the way downhill is very steep and awkward. Otherwise take the footpath from the stile by walking half-left (SW 235°) down a gentler slope to the road left of the house. Turn right and walk (N) alongside the road within the field to the signpost to the National Trust car park on the edge of the woods, just north of the house. The field of 'grey wethers' is on the left (W) of the road.

'Grey wethers' at Ashdown House
The most striking geological feature is the sarsen stones which lie scattered on the valley floor around Ashdown House, giving a good impression of what the whole of this downland must have looked like before it was cleared for arable cultivation. Most of the sarsen stones have now been dragged to hedge or parish boundaries, or they have been broken up and used in the walls or foundations of buildings. Here at Ashdown there are the full complement of stones, known locally as 'grey wethers', because from afar they look like a flock of grazing grey-white sheep.

Sarsen Stones, Ashdown House

The Landscape of Ashdown House

The historical landscape is interesting too. To begin with, underneath the woods surrounding Ashdown House there lie the intact outlines of the prehistoric and Romano-British field systems. On top of that, the deer park boundary can be clearly seen, which is a linear bank surrounding the wood. It dates from the 14th century, and was the Abbot of Glastonbury's deer-park here at Ashdown. The bank kept the deer in and they provided a fresh meat supply. Then, capping it, and now the most obvious piece of the landscape, are the woods which were planted with the house. The house was built during the period 1660–1665 by the first Earl of Craven. It was designed as a refuge for Elizabeth Queen of Bohemia (the Winter Queen), who lost her throne in 1620 and whose cause the Earl of Craven championed throughout a long and distinguished military career. The woods themselves date from the 17th century; there are some lime avenues, fragments of which originate from that date. There are vistas which are cut in the wood and which are very characteristic of late 17th and early 18th century woodland practice. The house, we thought, looks like a doll's house, with strong Dutch influence, set here among the Downs. (National Trust owned. Open Weds and Sat, April–Oct, tours only, 2.15pm, 3.15pm and 4.15pm). There is an explanatory notice board about the landscape in the car park.

Day Seventeen

ASHDOWN HOUSE TO SEVENHAMPTON

Ashdown House GR 284823 to Roves Farm, south of Sevenhampton GR 210887

With our last chance to enjoy the ridge-top views north and west, we walk into the seventh shire, Wiltshire, and from there descend to the springline villages of Bishopstone and Idstone. Here we pass our first pub on the route since West Ilsley, nearly 30 miles to the east. On the lowlands, the River Cole forms the county boundary. Near its banks, we pass through a fast-growing community forest to end with an opportunity for tea at Roves Farm.

Distance: 10.8 miles (17.3 km).

Maps: Explorer – 170 Abingdon, Wantage and Vale of White Horse.
                 Landranger 174 – Newbury, Wantage and surrounding area.

Transport: Swindon and District buses – Tel: 01793 33343, from Sevenhampton.
                 GR 207904.
                 Bishopstone, Ridgeway Explorer, bus stop at pond. GR 245836.

Taxis: Shrivenham   • Briant's Hire – Tel: 01793 782206.
                 Swindon   • Abbey Taxis – Tel: 01793 521666.
                                 • Radio Taxis – Tel: 01793 536666.
                                 • Highworth Link Radio Taxis – Tel: 01793 766666.

Car Parking: Ashdown House – in the National Trust car park.
                 Sevenhampton – in Roves Farm Visitor Centre car park.

Accommodation/Public Houses/Refreshments:
                 Bishopstone   • Cheney Thatch B&B – Tel: 01793 790508.
                                 • Prebendal Farm B&B – Tel: 01793 790485.
                                 • Royal Oak Public House and B&B, Cues Lane –
                                   Tel: 01793 790481.
                                 • True Heart Inn, High Street B&B and restaurant –
                                   Tel: 01793 790080.
                 Sevenhampton   • Roves Farm, B&B and teas – Tel: 01793 763939.
                 Highworth   • Chequers Retreat, B&B – Tel: 01793 766279.
                                   GR200925, 2.6 miles north of Roves Farm.

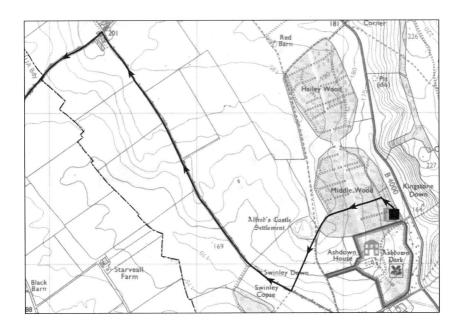

L eave **Ashdown House** car park on a wide footpath (NW) through the woods away from the house. At the first junction, turn left (W) up a gentle slope and cross a woodland ride on a north-south axis, cut through by the Earl of Craven in the 1660s. To your left Ashdown House is visible, perfect in its symmetry.

Cross the wide ride, continuing west to the edge of the wood (and the edge of the Abbot of Glastonbury's former deer park). Cross the stile in the wall which has been constructed from sarsen stones cleared from the fields. Go straight ahead over another stile to the ramparts (banks) of Alfred's Castle, a Pre-Roman Iron Age hill-fort. The ramparts were also constructed from piles of sarsen stones covered with turf. They measure about twelve feet from the bottom of the ditch to the top of the bank. Having had a look at the fort, turn left towards the house to a gate, stile and hunt jump with a track going south. *Do not* take this track, but instead bear right (SW 212°) across an open field towards an isolated wood. Before the wood and in the valley bottom, turn right (NW) onto a bridleway over Swinley Down. Soon, the open bridleway changes its nature to being curving and hedged. It shows all the classic characteristics of a sheep drove-way. It has small, linear, mounded boundaries with hedgerows but is very wide (40–50 feet); a vehicle track covers about a fifth of the width. We saw a wonderful mixture of butterflies and flowers here in July: meadow brown, ringlet and speckled wood butterflies, burdock, blue meadow cranesbill, goatsbeard (or 'jack-go-to-bed-at-noon'), yellow lady's bedstraw, hemp

Ashdown House from the south

agrimony, purple knapweed, field scabious, vetches, melilot and pink thistles, to name but a few. For one mile further north, climb the dip slope of the escarpment to the top. To the left (W) Swindon can be seen with its tower blocks and white-coloured Honda factory, and to the south-west, Charlbury Hill.

In the right-hand (E) hedge, which is mostly blackthorn, we saw several lichens on the upper branches in March. Lichens are indicators of good (unpolluted) air quality; they grow here as they obtain moisture from the prevailing south-westerly winds. While walking along this track we heard chaffinches, great tits, yellowhammers, dunnocks, robins and a wren.

On reaching the Ridgeway turn left (W) at some farm buildings. The Ridgeway is now at least 48 feet wide with pronounced 2–3 feet high linear mounds on either side.

The Ridgeway is broad and the present track only covers between a quarter and a fifth of its total original width. In prehistoric times, the track was even wider and was a more informal zone of communication (see day 14). When the Enclosure Acts in the 18th century divided up the Downs, arbitrary decisions were made which reduced the Ridgeway to its present width. This was when the linear mounds and hedgerows were made.

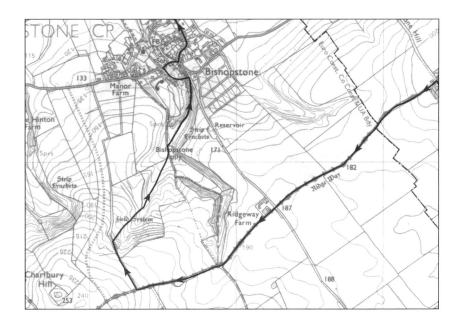

Ignore the footpath sign (NW) to Bishopstone. The first field boundary after joining the Ridgeway is reached at a gap in the hedge on the left, under a big beech tree. This hedge is the county boundary from Oxfordshire into **Wiltshire** (our seventh, and last, shire). By looking left (S) from here along the hedge, it is possible to see the notches made by the interlocking furlongs from the original open field system of the villages of Idstone and Bishopstone (see Day 4). We saw brown hares, fallow deer stags and lapwings displaying. In March, pairs of partridge were evident, rather than the covey of partridges that we had seen in December (Day 15).

Cross the road which leads down to **Bishopstone** as we are making a mile's diversion to the west side of Bishopstone in order to see some of the finest examples of strip lynchets in southern England.

If pressed for time, turn right and down this minor road to join our path by the millpond in Bishopstone.

The Seven Shires Way continues south-westwards along the Ridgeway.

Parish Boundaries

The minor roads are north-south ways meeting the Ridgeway and were used to connect the spring-line villages to the upland sheep pastures on the Downs. The parishes all along the edge of the escarpment in the Vale of White Horse are characteristically strip-shaped, arising from the days when each settlement had a mixture of upland and low-lying land, in the same way that the Anglo-Saxon farmers had a piece of the woodland in the Chilterns, (see Day 10). The hedgerows of these north-south routes are rich in flowering shrub species and are thought to be older than those of the Ridgeway.

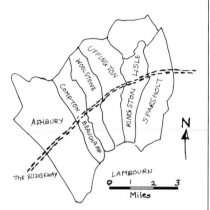

Parish boundaries on the Ridgeway

Ignore the wooden signpost and bridleways leading (N) and (S) at the next field boundary, instead continue 700 yards up the slope. Walk along the Ridgeway to just past the next field boundary on the right, where there is a stile before a metal gate. Cross this stile and bear half-right (032°) downhill into a deep dry valley in which lie remains of the strip lynchets (for an explanation of their formation, see Day 3). This is a permissive path, not a right of way. Continue in the base of the valley to a five-barred steel gate in the corner of this elongated field, to join the bridleway at Bishopstone Folly. Before crossing the stile next to the gate it is worth looking back at the strip lynchets. *Do not* take the bridleway going north along the ridge above the valley, but keep walking north-east in the base of the valley, again with fine strip lynchets to the right (E). Cross a stile at a gate and continue 100 yards to go through a metal kissing gate. Go down the right side of the valley and through another kissing gate onto a narrow path to the road.

Turn left to follow this minor road (Nell Hill) coming down from the Downs, and turn left (W) again at a fingerpost to Hinton Parva. After 10 yards, turn sharp left by a 'Give Way' sign down a narrow path into **Bishopstone**. Fork right, down concrete steps leading to a maze of paths between houses, built before cars and garages were invented. Turn left in front of some houses, follow the path downhill and bear right past a sculpture of fighting stags. Go over a bridge with white handrails and turn right and right again into a road (Oxon Place) by a large millpond. Turn right (NE). Predendal Farm (B&B) is along the road to the left.

Bishopstone

Bishopstone has several good examples of vernacular architecture. The early 19th century, three-storey mill is built of chalk blocks (the most common form of building material here), with brick quoins and a blue-slate, half-hipped roof. The road goes over the mill race (now not visible), from the dammed-up pond behind. There is a large fossilised ammonite embedded in the wall.

Another vernacular technique this village uses is sarsen and chalk block walls which are painted white and topped with thatch. Examples of this technique are in the house overlooking the millpond, in a row of former agricultural labourers' cottages and in some of the village walls.

Access Point: Bishopstone, 5 miles. Very limited parking in the village street called Hocker Bench. Pubs, telephone. GR 245837.

The village name means 'Bishop's ton' (ton = farm in Old English) and, in this case, was part of the estate of the Bishop of Salisbury. The origin of the street name 'Hocker Bench' is thought to derive from the place where the men crouched (dialect-*hocker*) while they waited to be hired for farm labour in the 1930s. Pass Cues Lane on the left (to Royal Oak PH). The pub sign shows a figure of King Charles II who took refuge in an oak tree after losing the Battle of Worcester in 1651.

Do not take Cues Lane but continue ahead uphill along the road called Hocker Bench and left at the chapel into High Street. Go past a thatched gable-end house and the True Heart Inn to pass a fine house on the right called 'Littlecot' whose central body was built in the 16th century. It has a sarsen stone foundation course two feet high, above that is chalk block. It is possible to see where the extension has been given brick quoins, and the roof has been raised to accommodate dormer windows.

Pass the road called The Wynchies and continue to where Cues Lane joins from the left into a road called 'The Forty'. Pass Forty Farm on the left, turn sharp right into New Town Lane, then after 200 yards, turn left (NE) along a footpath. We saw lambs in the fields here in March and a yellow brimstone butterfly enjoying the early spring sunshine. The pussy willow was out and a buzzard glided by.

Cue is the medieval name for the shoes of oxen, which looked like this.

We have seen the evidence of oxen ploughing that made the lynchets. So now we have another clue in 'Cues Lane'. All we need are some medieval oxen!

A double-gated footbridge over an enclosed ditch marks our entry back over the county boundary into **Oxfordshire**. Bear right (SE) and keep the hedge to your left to arrive at the back of Lower Idstone Farm. Go through the field gate, then turn left (NW) on reaching the minor road. This is the start of Featherbed Lane, perhaps called this because the mud in wet weather made it as soft as a featherbed! It is wide and curving, once again having the characteristics of ancient origins.

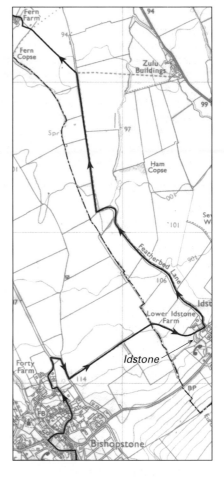

Walk for 0.75 miles, passing where the lane bears left and crossing some paving slabs that are part of a bridge, until you reach a steel five-barred gate. Turn right (N 354°) in front of the gate onto a footpath in the centre of a long narrow strip of woodland. There are remains of old elm stumps but also young elm saplings which are replacing them. Sadly, these may well suffer the resurgence of Dutch Elm disease which often recurs to hit trees after 10–20 years. Ancient, layered ash trees line the path. Ignore the first small gates on the left and right, but 0.75 miles further on, turn left through the gap in the hedge before the pond (GR 247860) and opposite a wooden gate on the right side. Away to the east is a farm named Zulu Buildings (see map) presumably to commemorate the Zulu War in 1879. Bear right (NW 315°) across a field to Fern Farm.

Enter the farmyard through a steel gate to the right of the farmhouse. Join a concreted track, and on reaching the first field boundary past the farm, the county boundary is only a field away to the left (W). Shrivenham church tower can be seen to the right. Cross the road beside some cottages with the Magdalen College coat of arms on their end wall (see also Day 10). Pass over three footbridges on a path towards the village of **Bourton**. Walk over a field where the soil is very sandy. Keep north-west across this field until a stile is reached in a wall, level with the chapel. Bear left across the field, with the remains of ridge and furrow ploughing, to the wall

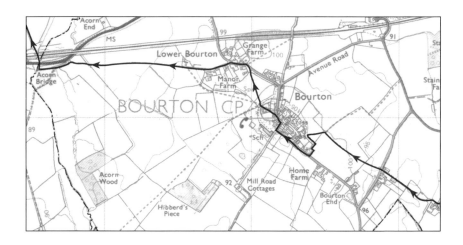

behind the houses. Then retrace your direction back south-east, so that you follow the wall around behind the chapel to emerge on the road immediately south of it. Turn right (NW) uphill past Bourton House. Bourton village is situated on top of a mound with fine views westwards, well away from the flood meadows. Bear right into the village centre and then left at the green, with an ancient cross and cast-iron pump, to the telephone box.

Access Point: Bourton, 8.5 miles. Telephone. GR 232870.

Victorian school building, Bourton

Bourton Grange

Fifty yards after the telephone box, turn left in front of some Victorian alms-houses, a school and school-house with a chapel behind. Pass in front of the manse, and turn right at the right-hand gate pier of Tower House onto a narrower footpath, which leads past the water tower and down the slope to cross a driveway. When we passed here in March, there was a carpet of aconites, snowdrops and crocuses with signs of wild garlic growing. Cross the stile opposite and bear right (345°) across the field to the right of Manor Farm. Leave the field by a kissing gate, and turn left onto a gravelled path beside the garden wall of Bourton Grange.

Follow the road left to a small triangular green. Turn left onto a farm track past Manor Farm, and onto a bridleway past the sewage works on the right. Only the ruined walls remain of Lower Bourton Farm. Continue (W) parallel to the London–Bristol railway. Brunel's triple-arched brick bridge is visible to the right. The soil is very sandy. Cross a bridge over a stream, then where a concrete track joins the bridleway from the right (N), turn right to emerge on the south side of the A420 Oxford–Swindon road. The fine, skewed, Brunel bridge is to the right (E). Turn left along the footpath for 200 yards, cross the road with care, and over the River Cole which forms the county boundary with Wiltshire at Acorn Bridge. Turn right (N) along the bridleway under the railway. Bear right (NE) past a rubbish tip (we have complained about this obstruction) and go towards a steel gate.

Now we enter part of the **Great Western Community Forest**.

Great Western Community Forest
The Great Western Community Forest is one of twelve such forests in England where local people, schools, businesses and community groups are working together to create a better environment. It covers 140 square miles in and around Swindon. A mosaic of woodland, green spaces and areas for wildlife are being created.
For more details contact Swindon Borough Council – Tel: 01793 466321.
www.forestweb.org.uk

Turn left here, and ignoring the black arrows that indicate a circular walk, keep left (W) of the River Cole and walk along the right (E) side of a long linear hedge. Keep north (341°) towards a plantation of osiers (willows). This is part of the Great Western Community Forest. Here, we were extraordinarily lucky to disturb a short-eared owl on the ground in broad daylight. Keep in the same direction over a concrete bridge at a tributary of the River Cole and along the asphalted road called 'Roves Lane', perhaps a derivation of 'Drovers Lane' from the days of sheep droving. At the old stone barn, keep ahead on the track towards **Roves Farm Visitor Centre** and car park.

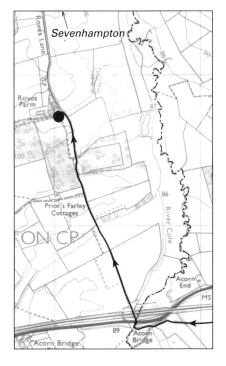

Day Eighteen

SEVENHAMPTON TO SOUTHROP

Sevenhampton GR 210887 to Southrop GR 200035

This is a longer stretch than usual, but much of the walking is on flat, straight roads or by the quiet banks of the meandering River Thames and its tributary, the River Leach, which form parts of the county boundary. At Buscot, we cross the Thames back into our first shire, Gloucestershire. This walk could be divided into two days by including visits to see the elegance of Buscot Park, experiencing the tranquillity of William Morris's home at Kelmscott Manor or hiring a boat on the River Thames at Lechlade. The 200 mile point is passed near to Southrop.

Distance: 14.8 miles (23.8 km).

Maps: Explorer 170 – Abingdon, Wantage and Vale of White Horse.
Outdoor Leisure 45 – The Cotswolds.
Landranger 163 – Cheltenham and Gloucester area.

Transport: Swindon & District buses – Tel: 01793 33343. Bus stop at Sevenhampton.

Taxis: Highworth • Link Cars – Tel: 01793 766666.
Lechlade • C T's Taxis – Tel: 01367 252575.
Faringdon • Shannon Cars – Tel: 01367 243510. Mobile 07971 191080.

Car Parking: Sevenhampton – Roves Farm Visitor Centre car park.
Southrop – in the lane on the west side of the Swan Inn, at the west end of the village.

Accommodation/Public Houses/Refreshments:
Coleshill • Radnor Arms PH – Tel: 01793 762366.
           • Mrs P Hoddinott, Ashen Copse Farm, B&B –
           Tel: 01367 240175.
Buscot   • Tea Shop – Tel: 01367 252142.
           • Apple Tree Guest House, B&B – Tel: 01367 252592.

Kelmscott • Plough Inn, B&B, lunches – Tel: 01367 850205.
Lechlade   • Lechlade Trout Fishery shop for snacks and drinks.
           • Cambrai Lodge, Oak Street, B&B – Tel: 01367 253173.
           • New Inn Hotel, Market Street – Tel: 01367 252296.
Southrop   • The Old Post Office, B&B – Tel: 01367 850231.

Accommodation list from Swindon Tourist Office – Tel: 01793 530328.
Camping facilities in Thames Path Companion – Tel: 01865 810224.

Rowing boats for hire on the River Thames. Riverside Boathouse, Lechlade –
Tel: 01367 253599.

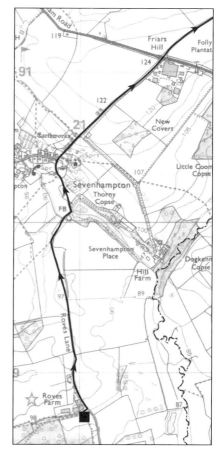

From **Roves Farm**, (south of **Seven-hampton**), walk north on the concreted lane passing fields showing the remains of ridge-and-furrow ploughing to the left, and Sevenhampton church ahead to the right. In the parkland behind the church there is a fine avenue of lime trees. On arrival at the village street, turn right to pass the entrance to the church and walk (NE) along the road towards Coleshill. Go straight ahead at the crossroads at Friars Hill, and continue along the minor road for 1.5 miles past Fresden Farm. There are wonderful views to the left over the Thames valley. Here we saw an extraordinary sight – a rat in the hedgerow eating the elderberries in late autumn. If hungry, rats will go to any length to find food!

The county boundary is to the right following the course of the River Cole. Our route does not follow the footpath nearer the boundary as access to it is along the narrow and busy B4508. At the left road bend at Fresden Barn, walk for 200 yards down the slope, turn right through a double-gated entrance onto a footpath across the field, in line

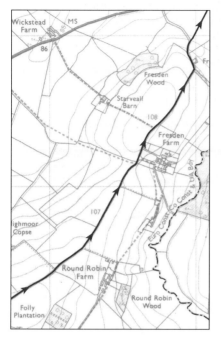

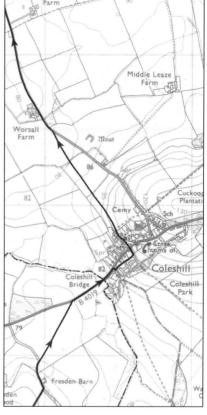

with the maring parlour on the left side of the village of **Coleshill**. Turn right at the road, and walk with care over the narrow bridge.

The River Cole forms the boundary between Wiltshire (nearside) and Oxfordshire (farside) and flows north-west to join the River Thames at St John's Bridge, Lechlade, as does the River Leach which we see later in the day.

Climb the slope into the village. Coleshill is built on the hill formed by the Corallian ridge of limestone above the clay Vale of White Horse. It is a typical estate village and its cottages are built of Cotswold stone and tile. Turn left at the remains of the former preaching cross. The 15th century church has some beautiful stained-glass windows, and memorials in marble and Coade stone (an artificial stone invented by Eleanor Coade in 1784). It has a trefoil-headed south door to the church tower, with crockets (leafy stone knobs) on the pinnacles and gargoyles.

Access Point: Coleshill, 3.8 miles. Shop, post office, pub, telephone. GR 236937.

Take the minor street just left of the church, and leave the village on the footpath heading in the same direction (NW) beyond a metal kissing gate. Walk, with the hedge on left, to a stile (332°). Go straight ahead through three fields. In the last field, walk towards Worsall Farm to join the road 100 yards before the farmhouse. Turn left onto the road and walk (NW) for 0.75 miles with views of Highworth to the left (W) and on to Snowswick Farm. Four hundred yards further on at Snowswick cottages, turn right onto a hedged footpath along a metalled drive to Broadleaze Farm. Follow the footpath signs, keep left of the farm buildings, then turn left again (N 014°). To the left the first glimpse of Lechlade church spire can be seen. Keep straight ahead (N) where the cart track bears away to the right (E). Keep along the footpath on the left side of the hedge, to cross under the power lines near the village of **Buscot**. Continue along the field edge; ignore the gap in the hedge on the right by the power line, but bear right out onto the Lechlade road opposite the former public house and tollhouse, passing the former limestone built forge to the left. Beware of the busy traffic. Turn right, then left (N) towards the village centre, past the Victorian Jubilee Hall built in 1897 and a water fountain.

Access Point: Buscot, 6.7 miles.
Shop, café, telephone, toilets, car park.
GR 231977.

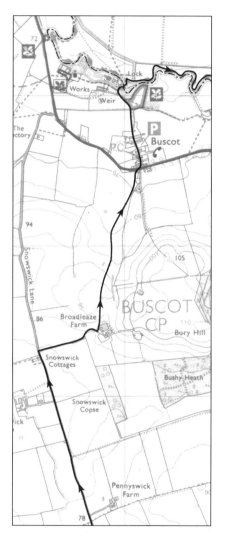

If time should allow, a visit to **Buscot Park** (GR 243969) with its 18th century house and beautiful Italianate water gardens is recommended. It is a mile diversion each way. Grounds open April–September, 2–6 pm, Mon–Fri (not BH). House open Wed–Fri and some summer weekends – Tel: 01367 240786. Teas served.

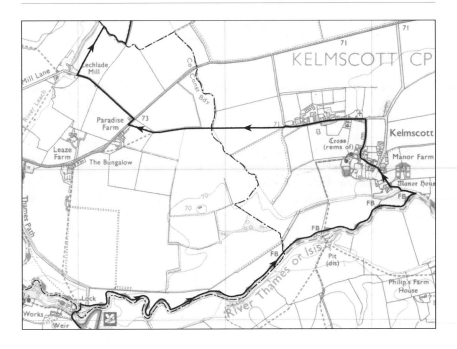

Continuing north, walk through the village where on the right is, allegedly, the first barn ever to be built totally of concrete dating from 1910. To the left is a 17th century, double-pile house. This means that the house is two rooms deep with a spine wall running down the middle. It is a splendid house with transom windows (with stone cross-bars) built about 1690. Pass the farmhouses and onto the footpath to Buscot Weir. Fork right on the concreted path, past a black, wooden-boarded building with a wheel inside (a former pump house) and cross the Buscot weir bridge into **Gloucestershire**. Turn right along a narrow path to the signposted National Trust Lock Cottage, in order to cross the Thames. After crossing the lock, turn right along the island, bear left over the footbridge off the island to the north bank, and turn right to walk downstream following the Thames Path. The River Thames here forms the county boundary between Oxfordshire (S) and Gloucestershire (N). 'En route', we pass more World War II 'pill-boxes'. On the river bank, in August, there were large clumps of pink Himalayan balsam with its exploding seed heads, the poisonous violet monkshood was in flower and the occasional, now quite rare, corn marigold, a tall plant with yellow flowers and serrated leaves. A mile from Buscot Weir, we cross a deep ditch with wooden hand gates either side; this is the county boundary. It leaves the river to route northwards. We leave Gloucestershire and enter Oxfordshire. The boundary is a thick, double hedgerow of hawthorns (the berries were red when we walked past in August) with a deep ditch. Continue along the riverbank past a footbridge over the river, and on for another 0.7 miles. On the left, the buildings of **Kelmscott** are visible in the distance; continue to where there is some woodland near the left bank of the river at GR 253987. This is where we leave the river by going through a grey gate, to bear left across a foot-bridge and turn sharp-left (W) onto a dirt track, past another 'pill-box' to head away from the river, and past the Manor House at Kelmscott. This was the home of William Morris, the designer and philanthropist. The house is privately owned but open to the public in summer (Weds, 11am–1pm, 2–5pm & some Sats 2–5pm). Telephone 01367 252486 for details. Teas served.

William Morris willow leaf design

Walk into the village where several of the cottages use vertical Cotswold stone slabs (known as 'planks') as fencing for gardens and fields.

There is a stone sculpture of William Morris on the wall of the Memorial Cottages to the left.

Access Point: Kelmscott, 9.0 miles. Pub, telephone. GR 250990.

Stone 'plank' fence, Kelmscott

An ancient preaching cross is on the grass verge near the Plough Inn. Leave Kelmscott by turning right at the pub and walking past the stone-built village hall. Turn left to pass the church on the right. William Morris and his wife are buried here. Their gravestone is at the far right end of the graveyard behind a bay bush. The church is interesting, having scratch dials and small consecration crosses on the right side of the porch arch, as well as medieval paintings in red ochre, and a window depicting St George slaying the dragon. Turn right out of the churchyard onto the road and out of the village to where the road turns sharp right. At the point of the turn, take a footpath straight ahead across the field (W 270°), *not* along the farm track, but towards the spire of **Lechlade** church in the distance. At a small brook, cross the county boundary back into Gloucestershire over a footbridge. From the brook, walk on in the same direction to reach a hedgerow in this L-shaped field. Walk on (W 278°), keeping close to left side of this hedgerow. At the second stile, bear away left from the hedge in the next field, towards the right side of Paradise Farm buildings. Cross the stile onto the Lechlade–Clanfield road. Turn right and then left down a minor road (NW) to Lechlade Mill. Before the 'tunnel' of trees around Lechlade Mill Cottage, and opposite the high wooden gates, turn right through the gap in the hedge and walk across the field (NE 034°). Head in the direction of a point halfway between the two far, left-hand power lines and the hedge to the left. This means walking parallel (50 yards away) to the hedge by the River Leach. The far side of the field boundary is a thick hedge with a ditch, and is the Gloucestershire/ Oxfordshire county boundary. At the footbridge (GR 232999) we cross back into Oxfordshire again. Turn right (E) on far side of this hedge to walk around the right perimeter of this field, with the hedge on our right, then turn right through a wide gap in the hedge. Walk on a grassy track (056°) to a corrugated-iron-roofed barn on the road. Turn left towards **Little Faringdon** and walk for a mile passing old, antlered oak and ash trees in the hedge.

Access point: Little Faringdon Church, 12.1 miles. GR 228014.

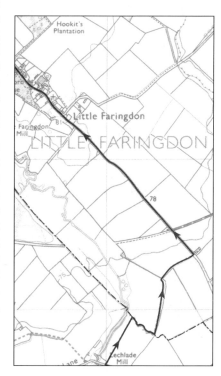

Little Faringdon church
There is a small and delightful church on the north side of the street. It has many features of Norman date, with a corbel table and a holy water stoup in the porch outside. Inside, the pillars are transitional Norman, with stiff-leaf foliage design. There is an Early English north aisle, a blocked north door and medieval glass. The Cistercian monks were famous for their farming. In the 13th century, granges were granted to the monks of Beaulieu Abbey in Hampshire, one of them being here at Little Faringdon.

Walk through the village beside the huge walls of Langford House and turn left (SW) around the corner of its grounds to walk on the footpath beside the busy A361 towards Lechlade. Just before the sign to the Lechlade trout fishery, and before the River Leach (hence Lechlade), cross the road with care and onto the footpath which goes along the right (N) bank of the River Leach.

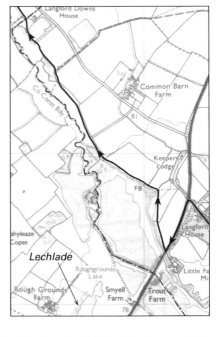

The map shows that the former course of the River Leach, before water management straightened it, forms the county boundary. Large, flooded, gravel pits are beyond the present river course. Follow the path alongside the river, past large, crack willow trees and young plantations of beech and oak being grown for the furniture trade.

Where a track crosses the river at a fording place (0.6 miles from road), turn right. After 50 yards, turn left to follow the left side of a field beside the wood. Go to the end of the field along the edge of an older wood, and go straight ahead through the gap in the hedge. A bridleway joins from the right. Continue on in the same direction on the right side of a wood, then follow a wire fence to a stile on the edge of Langford Downs House. Pass the lake to the right, then circle around the left perimeter of the tennis court to an ancient stone stile in a high hedge (the county boundary into Gloucestershire). Keep walking (NW 335°) along the left side of the next long field onto the minor road. It is here at GR 208035 that the 200 mile point is passed.

Crack Willow is so named because the twigs are very brittle allowing it to develop an unusual method of spreading far and wide. It usually grows near rivers, so that many of its broken twigs fall into the water to be carried away and buried in the mud of the bank downstream, where they can take root and grow into new trees.

Crack Willow by the River Leach

Turn left and at the road junction (ignore the footpath sign ahead) take the road left to **Southrop**, over the River Leach. On the right side are some wooden sluice gates, formerly used for water management in flooding the riverside meadows (see also Day 21). Follow the village street past the church, noting the start of the next day's section on a footpath leading right (N) between houses opposite Manor House Farm. Continue on to the Swan Inn, beyond which is a road to the right where there is space for car parking at the far (W) end of the village.

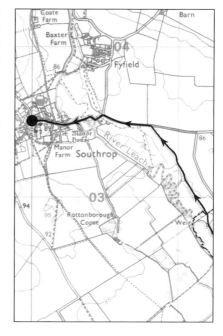

Day Nineteen

SOUTHROP TO GREAT BARRINGTON

Southrop GR 200035 to Great Barrington GR 210136

On the 'home stretch' northwards to Moreton-in-Marsh, we pass through small Gloucestershire villages. Ancient, thick hedgerows make up the county boundary. The building stone begins to reflect the fine quality Cotswold limestone beneath our feet.

Distance: 10.7 miles (17.5 km).

Maps: Outdoor Leisure – 45 The Cotswolds.
Landranger 163 – Cheltenham and Cirencester area.

Taxis: Burford • Fairways – Tel: 01993 823152.
• Mrs Jeacock – Tel: 01993 823337.
• Keylock – Tel: 01993 823230.

Car Parking: Southrop – in the road north of the Swan Inn, at the west end of village.
Great Barrington village hall car park, at south side of village.

Accommodation/Public Houses/Refreshments:
Eastleach Turville
• The Victoria PH – Tel: 01367 850277.
Little Barrington
• Fox Inn – Tel: 01451 844385.
• Inn for all Seasons, B&B and dinners – Tel: 01451 844324.

Burford Visitor Information Centre for accommodation in and around Burford –
Tel: 01993 823558 (open 10am–4.30pm Mon–Sat).

Southrop

The first record of the village is in the Domesday Book as Sudthropa or 'the Southern independent farmstead'. Up to the 1930s the village had a carpenter, an undertaker and a slaughterhouse, and up to 1947, a blacksmith. It now has a population of 220 (W L Cox, *Southrop in the Past*). A visit to the church just east of Manor Farm is well worthwhile. Externally, the herringbone design of the stones in the wall is Norman (11th century). There is a fine Norman font with a monument to John Keble, author of *The Christian Year*, after whom Keble College in Oxford is named. Locally, Southrop is pronounced 'Surrup' or 'Sowrup'.

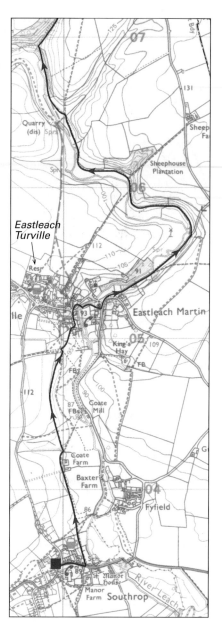

Walk east along **Southrop** village street, then just before a triangular green with a sign leading right to the church, turn left (N) onto a signed footpath just before a projecting house wall. Climb the two steep steps to go along an alley between houses.

Cross the traditional stone stile and continue northwards through the gates. On reaching a large field, keep straight ahead (N 350°) to another stile and towards the roof of a stone-built house. Keep ahead along the footpath, and pass left of the house along the right-hand edge of a field. Cross a footbridge and continue on (N 345°) to a stile on the brow of a small hill.

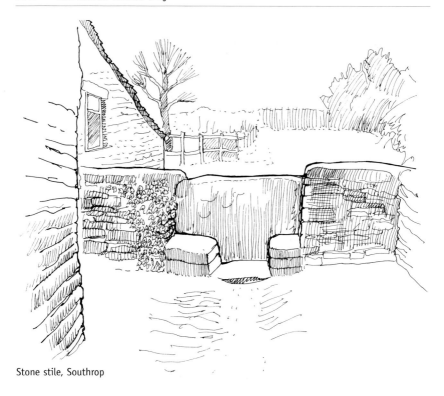

Stone stile, Southrop

Walk north along the top of the river cliff and by a wall above the meandering of the River Leach. This higher path would have been used in the winter, whereas the lower path would have been used in the summer or dry weather. This is a beautiful valley. We heard woodpeckers and fieldfares in October and saw a heron stalking frogs in the damp areas by the river. These two paths converge at a steel barred gate. Continue north to a stile with a yellow post which leads to a path between walls, left of the outskirts of the village of **Eastleach Turville**.

Access Point: Eastleach Turville, 1.25 miles. Pub, telephone. GR 201052.

At the end of the path, turn right onto a track, then left (N) onto a minor road that leads downhill past Verderer's Cottage. Turn right onto the main village street, then left by the telephone box at a house called Trout Beck. At the small triangular village green it is worth looking right, down to a small stone well.

Turn right across the clapper (i.e. stone-flagged) bridge. *Clapper* is the dialect for 'a rough or natural bridge across a stream; stepping stones'. Turn sharp left (N) immediately after crossing the brook to walk along the path beside the river into the churchyard of **Eastleach Martin**.

Leave Eastleach Martin churchyard by turning left (W) onto the road to the north of it. At the road junction, **Eastleach Turville**'s church with its saddleback roof is visible, with Eastleach Martin church just behind us. It is unusual how close together these two churches are. At the triangular green here, bear right (NE) towards **Holwell**, along the lower road, for 0.5 miles along the right bank of the River Leach.

When the road begins to ascend, turn left off the road into the Hathrop Estate and onto a marked footpath which follows the course of the river. Here we heard the loud cawing of jackdaws in October. Just after the first field boundary, keep right of a large ash tree to continue following the track. On the opposite bank there are prominent river cliffs. Keep on the right (E) side of the river at the base of the hill and walk towards the bottom of a wood, through a five-barred gate, and keep to the path on the river-side of a stone wall. At a point where the path is very near the river bank, cross over the stile, and walk on the uphill side of a wire fence along the field edge parallel to the river. At the end of this field, there is a broken down stile in its corner. Continue on towards the long, triangular-shaped wood ahead and over another stile. Watercress and water-mint grow among the grass, indicating the dampness of this meadow, with water forget-me-not in the clear water of the river. Here, we heard the song of linnets feeding on seeds in May.

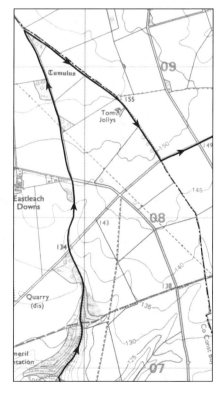

A bridleway from Eastleach Turville joins here at a stone clapper bridge. Follow the right (E) side of the river and enter the wood, where we saw a colony of rats taking the pheasant food! There were violets, celandine, wood avens and the green spathes of cuckoo pint. A buzzard flew just over our heads as if to investigate us. Its wings were at full stretch with primary feathers spread like fingers. Where the footpath enters a field on the right, keep on along the bottom of the field (N 345°) and continue along the bridleway with an iron fence on the left. Bear right (NE) along the left (eastern) inside-edge of the wood and start to climb gently at GR 198069 (N 036°). Where a track crosses the path keep straight on. The track is Akeman Street, the Roman road which we crossed on Day 7 when travelling to Ludgershall.

When our path emerges from the wood between two fields, cross a track, bear right, then left, to walk along the left (NE) woodland edge to the road. A late-in-season peacock butterfly feeding before hibernating for winter floated by us, and scarlet pimpernel and blue speedwell were still flowering in October. Cross the road and go across the field (N 005°) on the bridleway.

Walk on the right (E) side of a small wood within a limestone wall; it is made of thin-layered stones which come from the weathered surface of the rock and were gathered from the surrounding fields to build walls. We saw dark-green spurge laurel here, so typical of chalk and limestone woods.

A scared rabbit
A close brush with a rabbit: as we were walking and chatting we frightened a rabbit, which, in its confusion to run in any direction, ran between the boots of one of our party, which made her the second startled creature!

Cross a farm road and continue on (NNW) along the left (W) side of a wall, and under the power lines to pass another small wood. It was a mass of bluebells and pink campion in May.

The tumulus marked on the map is just north of this wood, but no signs of it remain today, except a dark patch in the soil on the ploughed field. This would have been a good site, high up on top of the Cotswolds plateau, and it is significant that it lies near the county boundary.

Walk on beside a stone wall and woodland to where there is a waymark and an opening in the wall. Turn right here, then sharp right again (SE 125°) to walk back in almost the same direction. This track is the Gloucestershire/Oxfordshire boundary and is very impressive at this point. There are two walls, thirty feet apart, lined by thick hedgerows, where we saw cowslips growing.

Continue to walk south-east with Oxfordshire to the north and Gloucestershire to the west.

Tom Jollys
This house sits on the county boundary and the tale goes that the local school children used to beg their parents to live there, since, as they would be living in neither county, there would be no need for them to attend school!

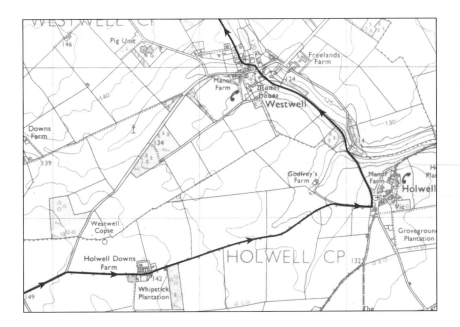

Walk past the house Tom Jollys, to the minor road. Turn left towards **Westwell**. Walk straight across the small crossroads, then 350 yards ahead, bear right onto the bridleway to Holwell Downs Farm. Pass by the group of fine farm buildings. Mrs Jeacock (see taxis) used to live here in the 1930s as her father was the herdsman. There were also a carter and a shepherd but the farmer lived off-site.

The stone-built implement sheds on the right are a fine example of pre-garage days. The barn on the left also gives an indication of pre-mechanised times. It has left and right bays for grain and threshed straw. In the middle was a threshing floor between the two large doors which, when opened, provided wind to winnow the grain. Many of these barns were fitted with a threshing machine at the back, first driven by steam, then by oil engines and some by electricity, before being made redundant by the invention of the combine harvester.

Follow the bridleway (E) for one mile. This is a high, lonely stretch of land where skylarks sing from far above. By the wayside in autumn we saw the rich bronze of comma and striking red of red admiral butterflies. On meeting the road turn left to **Holwell** church.

Holwell and Westwell do not refer to wells in the modern sense, but to springs (Anglo Saxon *wielle* = spring). Pits were dug to recover the spring water.

Access Point: Holwell, 7 miles. Telephone, car parking very limited. GR 233090.

At the church, bear left (NW) on the road to **Westwell**. Walk for 0.25 miles downhill then, at a sharp right corner, continue straight ahead on the footpath across a field. Keep to the right of the wood (345°) and bear left to walk along the valley bottom to Westwell. On reaching two gates onto a drive, cross the drive and walk into the garden on the left side of the brook. Go left of the line of houses to pass behind a house on the right, through a yard, and onto a drive to exit at the fingerpost by the war memorial. This memorial is in memory of two brothers killed in the First World War: the brass numeral was part of the medieval clock on the Cloth Hall at Ypres.

Access Point: Westwell, 7.7 miles. Telephone, car parking very limited. GR 224100.

At Westwell, the most westerly spring in Oxfordshire feeds the village pond. There is a manor house, preaching cross and church. The church is well worth visiting and has a fine 17th century monument inside and bale tombstones outside.

War Memorial, Westwell

Bale tombstones, Westwell churchyard

Take the path uphill on the right side of the church and leave at the rear of the graveyard. Bear left on a path between stone walls and onto an open green at the back of a barn. Turn right (N) on a track between a stone wall and a fence. At the end of the wood make a 'dog-leg' right then left, to follow the route of the d'Arcy Dalton Way, the long distance footpath on which we walked on Day 3 in the north of the county. Keep to the left (W) of the hedge and about three-quarters of the way along the field, and 25 yards on from a pale, decayed tree-trunk in the hedgerow, there is a grey, steel hand-gate. Go through this and turn left to walk along the right side of the hedgerow for 100 yards. Continue north-west at the next field entrance, along the left of the stone wall, and

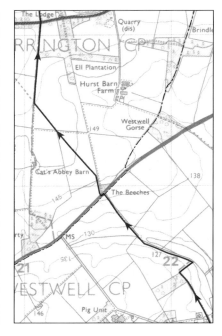

uphill to the B4425 Burford/Bibury road. On this field edge we saw another late-in-season peacock butterfly in October, the last scabious flowering and the shiny-red, poisonous berries of white bryony. Cross the road, which follows the line of the county boundary, and enter **Gloucestershire** by continuing (NW) on the track. Having just passed the small wood by the road, walk on the left side of the hedge and continue for 100 yards from the hedge gap. There, bear left (NW 325°), aiming just right of the opposite left-hand diagonal corner of the field. There is a waymark here. Cross the cart-track at this far corner of the field and continue in the same direction (325°) to the far side of the field, where there is a white-painted way-mark. *Do not* continue along the footpath across the next field, but bear right (N) on a grassy bridleway towards the A40 Burford/Cheltenham road. Cross the A40 to walk north-west on the bridleway. This path crosses a strip of high land and underneath the surface is a very high quality limestone. All along the hillside at Taynton (see Day 20), Sherbourne and the Barrington villages, there is a series of quarries producing this close-grained freestone (so named since it could be cut in any direction), which was in great demand until the 18th century. The path descends to **Little Barrington** church which is built of fine smooth ashlar lime-stone. Outside the church, on the right side of the porch, is a sculpture, a classi-cal tablet of 1702. On the opposite (N) outside wall, there is a re-set tympanum (a semi-circular or drum shaped stone) showing two angels adoring Christ. The block of stone in the churchyard is the remains of a preaching cross.

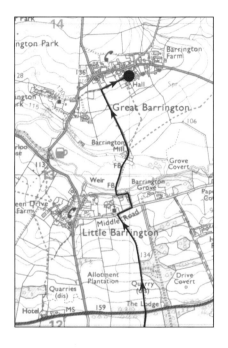

Access Point: Little Barrington Church, 9.9 miles. Telephone. GR 209127.

Turn right at the church, and just before the large house of Barrington Grove, turn left (N) down the high-walled lane and curve left past the cottages to turn right (N) across the wooden footbridge over the swift flowing River Windrush.

The river banks were dotted with golden-yellow marsh marigolds or kingcups in early March. Walk north through the flood meadows. It is worth looking back right to see Barrington Grove. Cross over another bridge to Barrington Mill with its large millpond and mill leat on the left.

Bridge over the River Windrush, Little Barrington

A mill is sited at a point where it is possible to tap into the power generated by a fall of water. To create this artificially, a stream is dammed and a millpond is formed. To ensure a sufficient 'head' of water, the water is taken off a stream some distance away and led through a mill leat or embanked channel. Here it is stored at the rear of the mill and led over a 'race' to drive the wheels. The water then joins the stream by means of the 'tail race'.

Do not take the footpaths at their junction north of the mill, but turn half-left (NW) to the village street of Great Barrington. Walk up the track and turn right along the narrow lane before the village buildings to the village hall car park. Alternatively, it is possible to continue up the track to turn right at the war memorial. Follow the village street for 250 yards, past the telephone box and on for a further 10 yards, to take a winding alley going right, down to the village hall car park. The only car access to this is from the lane along the south side of the village.

Day Twenty

GREAT BARRINGTON
TO BLEDINGTON

Great Barrington GR 210136 to Bledington GR 244228

We make more progress towards our northern destination across high farmland, through small Cotswold stone villages, with tales of highwaymen, and an ancient lane towards Bledington.

Distance: 10 miles (16 km).

Maps: Outdoor Leisure – 45 The Cotswolds.
Landranger 163 – Cheltenham and Cirencester area.

Transport: Rail – Kingham station 1 mile from Bledington – Oxford/Worcester line.

Taxis: Burford (for Great Barrington)
• Fairways – Tel: 01993 823152.
• Mrs Jeacock – Tel: 01993 823337.
• Keylock – Tel: 01993 823234.
Bledington   • Robin Oldridge – Tel: 01608 658495.
Mobile: 07850 266903.

Car Parking: Great Barrington – near the village hall car park on the south side of the village.
Bledington – on the edge of the village green.

Accommodation/Public Houses/Refreshments:
Fifield   • Merrymouth Inn, Stow Road, B&B, coffees & lunches –
Tel: 01993 831652.
• Merryfield, High Street, B&B – Tel: 01993 830517.
Nether Westcote
• Cotswold View Guesthouse, B&B, lunches & teas –
Tel: 01993 830699.
• New Inn, lunches (not Mon), summer campsite –
Tel: 01993 830827.
Bledington   • King's Head Inn, B&B, lunch & dinner –
Tel: 01608 658365.
• The Old Forge, B&B (no suppers) – Tel: 01608 658337.

Foscot	• The Old Stores – Tel: 01608 659844
	(0.5 miles from Bledington).
Bould	• Bould Farm, B&B – Tel: 01608 658850
	(1.5 miles from Bledington).
	• Cobweb Cottage, Bould, B&B – Tel: 01608 658036.
Kingham	• Tollgate Inn & restaurant – Tel: 01608 658389
	(1.5 miles from Bledington).

Burford Visitor Centre – Tel: 01993 823558 (10am–4.30pm, Mon-Sat) for comprehensive list of accommodation.

Face north towards **Great Barrington** village in the road by the village hall car park. Turn right on this road for 50 yards, then left up a winding alley between cottages to join the village street. Turn right, and after 200 yards turn left (opposite the blacksmith's forge and village notice-board on the right), along a wide concrete track (N). In the recess on the left side of the start of the track is a small tap and a little stone basin. This was formerly a communal source of water. Walk on for 300 yards, and turn right (E) behind the farm buildings. Where the track divides in front of an asbestos-roofed barn, turn left (N) through the five-barred steel gate onto a track. The path crosses a small valley and passes under a group of ash trees. On the right (E) side of the path a stream comes through the dam. It is here left of the top of the causeway that a damp area can be seen which was formerly a large fishpond. The path continues uphill, along a hollow way northwards (016°). Cross through another steel gate.

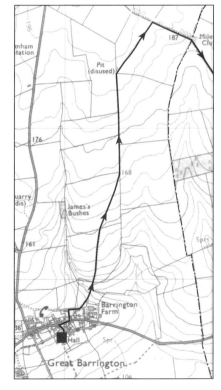

At the first field hedge, the path has been diverted first right then left around the eastern side of the field. The farmer was growing flax in this field in June and he had planted wild poppy seed around the edge: the blue of the flax flowers with the red of the poppies looked marvellous. There were also skylarks singing at the next field hedge. The spire of **Burford** church below is visible if you

Broomrape

We were excited to find the increasingly rare broomrape growing beside the track. Broomrapes are a group of highly specific parasitic plants with each species devoted to parasitising one plant genus, such as broom (hence its name), gorse, clover, thyme or even ivy. The broomrape does not have any chlorophyll of its own to make energy from sunlight like most plants, but throws up brown or reddish flower spikes from its underground roots as they attack the root nutrient highways of these other plants to become their source of food. Beautiful, azure, Common Blue butterflies abound here on warm summer days in June.

look across the valley to the right (SE). Walk northwards but on the right (E) side of the hedge along a well-defined track. Delicate pink dog-roses and cream elder flowers adorned the hedge. We also admired the field edges. Either the farmer only sprayed the centre of the fields or had planted wild flowers, as there were heartsease (the wild pansy) and ox-eye daisies in bloom. In early November, these hedgerows were full of wild bird food and were ablaze with colour: field maple leaves a pale gold, bryony berries a shiny red, scarlet red rosehips, and the hawthorn berries a rich claret colour. These hedges provide a rich wildlife habitat and greatly increased our enjoyment as walkers. Pass by a patch of stinging nettles, which covers what was a disused pit, and follow the diverted footpath westwards along the hedge boundary to the clump of beech trees at the end of the shelter belt. Turn right (SE) on the track under the trees. At the end of the shelter belt where there is a waymark, there is another group of beeches (Miletree Clump) on the county boundary. Cross into **Oxfordshire** from **Gloucestershire** and continue south-east past a deserted farmhouse and outbuilding. Looking half-right (S), the Berkshire Downs and the Ridgeway are visible from here on a clear day. Scabious and knapweed were flowering abundantly in June. After 300 yards, turn sharp left (NE) to follow the left side of the hedge on the bridleway to Tangley Farm.

Taynton Quarries

From this vantage point, about a mile away across the valley to the right (E), an area of woodland, grassy humps and bumps, broken ground, and an old rusty winch can be seen. This is the site of the once famous Taynton quarries of one of the finest oolitic limestone freestones of the Middle Ages. Stone from here was used for the Oxford colleges, and also was transported, via the River Thames, to be used at Windsor Castle and St Paul's Cathedral.

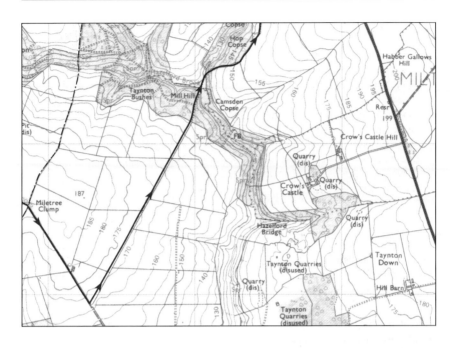

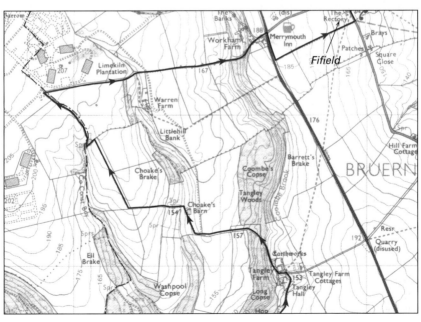

Walk for nearly a mile (NE) and enter Mill Hill woods. We saw buzzards and red kites circling above here. Walk downhill to cross Hazelford Brook where we saw a heron standing stock still, fishing. Leave the track and bear right on the footpath on the right edge of the field, cross Coombe Brook to the right, and go up the steep slope to the southern edge of the Hop Copse. There are indeed wild hops in the wood, with hazel coppicing and evidence of layering of the old ash trees in the woodland boundary. Sloe berries were ripening and hazel catkins, half an inch long, were forming ready for spring when we walked by in November. Descend to walk around the right (E) side of Tangley Hall. Having reached the gate, it is worth looking back to see a small outbuilding situated up on the slope behind the house. This was formerly a conduit house in which water, collected at a higher level, can be piped to the 17th century Tangley Hall below.

Turn left onto the farm road and into the farmyard of Tangley Farm. Pass a former hay barn with a stone external staircase leading up to the loft. A stony bank by this barn was abundant with wild flowers in June, with deep-blue meadow clary, yellow mullein, the purple of hedge woundwort, the orangey-pink of sainfoin, the pink common mallow and purple thistles all growing together. Walk northward over an old, stone sluice bridge over Coombe Brook, where earthworks to the right are marked on the map. These could have been a former watermill, as indicated by the low meadows, the remains of a millpond and the woods named Mill Hill. Continue north-west up the slope through Tangley woods and then westwards. In June, the pink meadow cranesbill flowers were growing by the wayside.

Tangley Hall Conduit House

Tom, Dick and Harry
In the late 18th century, Burford was the headquarters of the notorious Dunsdon brothers — gamblers, fighters and highwaymen. Three of the four brothers, Tom, Dick and Harry, planned to rob Tangley Hall (Lone Farm, as it was called by the locals), but the brothers were expected and a trap was laid. As Dick slipped his arm through the shutter of the door to slide back the bolt, the constable grasped it and tied the hand to the catch. Dick, refusing to be captured, shouted to his brothers, 'Cut! Cut!', and they did so – by severing his arm at the elbow with their swords! Dick died of his wound; Harry and Tom were hanged on an oak tree at the village of Fulbrook nearby.

Pass through two steel gates (GR 229172), then bear right onto an ancient track (NW 340°), down the slope past what was Choake's Barn (no longer standing). Bear left (W) over a stone-culverted brook. The water-loving flower, ragged robin, was growing there. Go uphill, past the spring on the right (N) side of the track. There are a series of small valleys here with a line of springs where water in the porous limestone is impeded by the impervious clay layer and so appears at the surface. Walk up to the top of the slope, turn right (NW) to walk with some of the **Little Rissington** airfield hangars on the left. It is said that during the Gulf War in 1992, the Rissington hangars were put into a state of readiness to act as a temporary hospital for the expected casualties. Operating theatres and beds were ready but were not needed as there were few casualties. Lapwing, buzzards and hares can be seen on this high land.

Continue on the bridleway to the end of the field, turn sharp left for 50 yards, then right through the gap in the field boundary. A thick multi-specied hedgerow comes up to this corner from the south. It is the county boundary and the same hedge that we crossed earlier at Miletree Clump. Walk north, in **Oxfordshire**, beside the stone wall (the county boundary), with **Gloucestershire** on the far side. Near the airfield buildings the county boundary goes straight ahead continuing its path northwards. The bridleway also continued ahead prior to its closure by the building of the airfield in 1937 as the prospect of war loomed. Turn right (E) along the bridleway. Pass a very overgrown concrete sentry box, past the end of Limekiln Plantation, whose name is an indication of former industry here, to pass the entrance on the right to Warren Farm. Continue downhill (E) into a green lane, across a causeway over a small stream, and climb towards the A424 Burford to Stow-on-the-Wold road, passing Workham farm to the left. The Merrymouth Inn is named after a local French family, the Murimuths, who were important landowners. Someone, quite recently, tried to change the name to Hunters Lodge, but a 'fisticuffs' almost ensued, so the name reverted back to the Merrymouth Inn!

Access Point: Merrymouth Inn, Fifield, 6 miles. GR 233185.

Turn right (S), past the Inn. Walk alongside the road for 200 yards then, at the first field boundary on the left, turn left (E) at the waymark. Follow a narrow bridleway on the right side of the hedge to the village of **Fifield**. Here we saw a bumble-bee feeding on the last knapweed flowers in November. Turn left (N) at the lane and after 100 yards take the first street right indicated 'Fifield only'. The name of the village of **Fifield** is derived from 'five hides' (approximately five hundred acres) so was previously called *Fyfthide.*

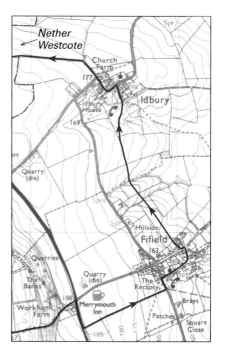

Ignoring the footpath sign across the churchyard, continue ahead from the church gate to descend the village street. A village wall well (see Idbury wall well, page 187) is situated on the right side, and on the left Cotswold stone slabs placed vertically form the garden wall of the cottages. Turn left at the Manor and the triangular green, pass by another wall well. At a second triangular green, turn left to start ascending the street, but opposite Corner Cottage is a waymark and an iron kissing gate leading to a narrow footpath. Turn right along this narrow path to cross a wildflower meadow (NW 324°) towards **Idbury**. Go through six fields and over two footbridges across small streams. In the third field, the remains of the ridge-and-furrow cultivation are very evident on walking up and down across the ground. This was probably part of the open field system of Idbury. Bear half-right in this field

---

Fifield church

The stone-spired church is interesting. The octagonal spire rises directly from an octagonal tower. The trefoil-headed bell openings were added in the 14th century. Inside, the chancel is 13th century and there is a medieval glass window on the south side, with two shields in the glass. Above the shield is a 'sun of splendour' in black and yellow glass. Surrounding the shield are 'crowns in thorns', which, apart from their religious significance, commemorated Henry VII's victory over Richard III at the Battle of Bosworth in 1485 when the English crown is said to have been found in a thorn bush.

The 'crowns in thorns' window, Fifield church

towards an old oak tree, cross the stile and keep to the right side of the hedge. In the field immediately below Idbury, the path follows the ancient track between the ridge-and-furrow and bears right (E) across the field in line with the church. In the wall, before the kissing gate, there is another wall well.

> **Idbury wall well**
> Originally there was a spring coming out of the hillside, but to make it accessible to animals the farmers built a retaining wall so that the water was able to fill a stone basin, which now no longer exists. Today the watery patch has water-mint growing in it.

Go through the kissing gate, and turn left along a path between a hedge and a garden wall. At the village street turn left (W), unless you wish to divert 50 yards to the right to visit the church.

Walk west along the village street to Idbury House on the corner. The house has three storeys, is double piled (see page 165) and probably dates from the late 17th century. It has a roundel above the central window with an inscription, 'Oh, more than happy countryman, if he but knew his good fortune.'

Ignore the footpath pointing SW at the corner, but go right (NW) on a minor road out of the village towards Westcote. Travel 0.6 miles. At the end of the first field boundary to the left, the county boundary is crossed again, this time from **Oxfordshire** into **Gloucestershire**. Here, it is a small, single specied hedge and is not particularly impressive. The old ash tree also seems to be the boundary marker. At this point the county boundary turns left to follow the road, then right (N) at the next field boundary so making a 'notch' in its route. The only likely reason (as in Day 4) is that a furlong block of the former open field system was the origin of the boundary.

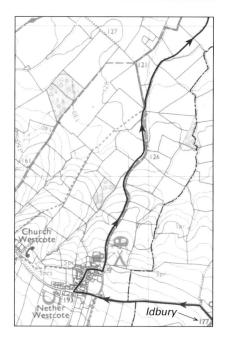

Continue into the village of **Nether Westcote**. Turn right at the triangular green with the village notice board, but beware of the dangerous corner! Pass the Cotswold Tea Rooms to the left and go downhill alongside the wide village green to continue on the road as it bends right. Pass Manor Barn House and the New Inn public house to where the road turns right and goes uphill.

Access Point: Nether Westcote, New Inn, 8 miles. GR 226204.

Turn sharp left (N) from the road into an ancient hollow way with huge stumps of former elm trees in the banks. This bridleway can be very muddy, so 150 yards on there is a stile and an option of taking the footpath immediately to the left (W) parallel to the bridleway. The woodland banks of the hollow way with its curving route indicate that it was wider in former times, possibly an ancient link between the Westcotes and **Bledington**. Hartstongue fern and another bushier one (hard fern) grow here, interspersed with wild angelica plants. The county boundary is to the right (E) following the course of a small tributary of Westcote Brook which is crossed further on. Walk for 0.75 miles from the start of the way, over a small brook where it is culverted under the track. A footpath joins from an open field on the left at GR 229214. Ignore this sign and continue on the bridleway between hedges for only 50 yards. Then turn right, over both a small stile in the hedge and a footbridge, to go through scrub area on a well-defined path (N 024°) for 300 yards, with a stream on the right side. Leave the scrub area by a wooden hand-gate and over a woodland bank into a meadow. The path now bears more to the right (E 055°). In the first field keep near the left (W) side of a small brook, then walk through the

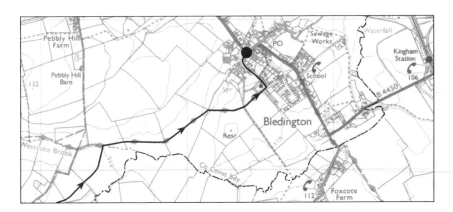

middle of the next two fields (030°). At the Westcote Brook, which forms the county boundary, turn right (E) and walk beside the brook on the **Gloucestershire** side of it. We have joined the Oxfordshire Way, a 65 mile-long footpath from Bourton-on-the-Water in Gloucestershire to Henley-on-Thames in Oxfordshire. In this first field in Gloucestershire, bear left away from the brook by walking due east across two fields with footbridges. In the third field, follow the right side of a hedge up a gentle slope and past a former windpump. Cross the lane and go to Bledington church through an extension to the cemetery.

Bledington church is magnificent and benefited from the wealth of the wool trade. Its most noticeable features are its double clerestory windows and a tiebeam roof. There is a fine 15th century painted glass window of St George slaying the Dragon. The name Bledington was derived from *Bladening ton* which in Old English means, 'farmstead on the River Bladen'. The River Bladen was the earlier name for the River Evenlode.

Turn left (NW) past the church onto the road downhill, past some more vertical Cotswold-stone slab fences, to arrive at the large village green with the Kings Head Inn situated in the NW corner of it. For the shop, post office and telephone, turn right to walk beside the village green to the street corner.

Day Twenty-one

BLEDINGTON TO
MORETON-IN-MARSH

Bledington GR 244228 to the Four Shire Stone near
Moreton-in-Marsh GR 230322

*The River Evenlode, on its quiet, meandering course towards the Thames, first
forms the boundary, which then strikes across higher land. We pass through
villages where the reddish marlstone has been used. At Moreton-in-Marsh the
watershed is near with the Severn Valley to the north and the Thames basin to
the south. After 232.3 miles, we complete the circuit at the Four Shire Stone.*

Distance: 11.2 miles (18 km).

Maps: Outdoor Leisure 45 – The Cotswolds.
Landranger 163 – Cheltenham and Cirencester area.
Landranger 151 – Stratford-upon-Avon and surrounding areas.

Transport: Rail – Kingham station, 1 mile from Bledington, on
London/Oxford/Moreton-in-Marsh line – Tel: 0845 7484950.

Taxis: Bledington • Robin Oldridge – Tel: 01608 650852.
Mobile: 0850 266903.
Moreton-in-Marsh
• Cotswolds Taxis – Tel: 07710 117471.
• Town and Country Taxis – Tel: 01608 674477.

Car parking: Bledington – beside the village green.
Moreton-in-Marsh – parking is possible in the minor roads of the housing
estate, north of the A44 (GR213324), on the eastern edge of the town.

Accommodation/Public Houses/Refreshments:
Moreton-in-Marsh for accommodation (see Day 1).

Tourist Information Centre – Tel: 01608 684621, no other refreshments or
accommodation on the route.

From **Bledington** village green, walk along Chapel Street, past University Farm to the left, with its steeply pitched roofs, and continue along the lane to the house at the end. Turn right, then left along a footpath. On entering the field, keep along the left hedgerow. After 100 yards, bear slightly right across the field (NE 050°) to a footbridge across a dyke, then continue in the same direction (050°) to a dismantled railway.

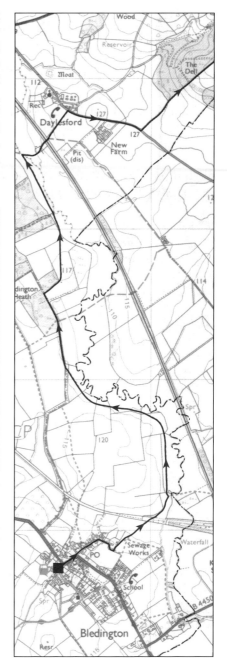

Railway Embankments

The speed with which dismantled railways acquire a growth of vegetation is quite extraordinary. This embankment on the edge of the field is covered in tree-sized hawthorns resembling an old hedge boundary, but in fact can only be about 35 years old at the most. These disused lines (this one a former ironstone route from Banbury to South Wales), can become long linear nature reserves — valuable by connecting one habitat with another, thus ensuring the healthy continuation of species.

Cross the railway, climb the bank, then bear right, and keep to the left hedge of a narrow field to a corner. Bear away from the hedge to a field gate and stile between two large trees close to the River Evenlode. *Do not* take the foot-bridge across the river at the Gloucester-shire/Oxfordshire county boundary, but walk (N) parallel to the left hedge in the second field. Here we are walking the ridges and furrows of the medieval cultivation where the plough reached as near to the river as possible. Cross the stile beside the next field gate, again near the River Evenlode.

An extract from Hilaire Belloc's verse aptly describes this quiet corner of the world – 'Quietly flows the Evenlode, forgotten in the western wolds' – the only interruption to the peace being the occasional train on the Oxford/Worcester railway line. There were spikes of purple loosestrife, pink great willow herb and the small pink flowers of vervain growing here in August. The meanders of the Evenlode are so convoluted at this point that the river could, one day, form an ox-bow lake.

After this stile, the map shows the footpath to the left side of the hedge of the next field, but the waymarks guide us to walk along the right side of the hedge through another steel gate very near the river, and along the right side of a fence, between it and the river in the next field. Continue to follow the path approximately parallel to the river then, in the last field before the wood, go straight ahead to the far corner to cross a stile onto an ancient track. Turn right to join it.

The Track to Bledington Heath
This is a green lane which would formerly have been much wider, as evidenced by a line of ancient oak trees and coppiced trees further into the woodland. There are boundary banks and ditches on both sides. In the woodland is more evidence of the medieval fields, for as we walk, we cross undulations in the track which are alternately dry and wet — the ridges and furrows of the ploughing. We found a badger's print in a muddy patch.

After 350 yards, ignore the wooden gate on the bridleway to the right, but 200 yards further on, at the entrance of an area where there is woodland on both sides, turn right to cross the stile. Keep to the woodland edge, just right of the barbed-wire fence. We heard the squawk of a little owl here in hot, sunny, August weather. These owls hunt during the day so can sometimes be seen but more often are heard. At the corner, bear left away from the wood across the middle of the field, aiming just to the right of **Daylesford** church spire (N 003°). Cross the footbridge in the far diagonal corner hedge. Continue along the right edge of the next field for 25 yards, then go through a gap to continue in the same direction, but on the right side. Keep to the right (E) edge of the wood called Lower Oddington Ashes, to walk along the left bank of the river, where we saw a heron in these damp meadows. Just before the bridge, on the far bank, is a cattle-watering hole where the ground is 'poached' (i.e. made into mud by the hooves). Turn right over the footbridge and bear half-right (SE 100°) towards a gate. Bear left up the cart-track.

Sluice Gate, Daylesford

On passing a field gate to the left of the cart-track, a wooden sluice gate is visible in the small brook. This is the remains of a former water management system. By inserting a handle, called a key, to the mechanism the gate was lowered or raised to control the water levels of the brook downstream.

Continue over the railway bridge and through a gate. Walk on the right side of the hedgerow towards Daylesford village road.

Access Point: Daylesford church, 2.6 miles. Telephone, limited parking. GR 243259.

Turn right onto the road, passing on the left the edge of the parkland of Daylesford House. Pass New Farm to the right, then after 150 yards turn left onto the bridleway.

At this turning the church tower of Churchill can be seen ahead (SE). It is a three-quarter size replica of the tower of Magdalen College in Oxford.

On walking along this farm road in Gloucestershire, the county boundary is the straight hedge a field away to our right. Keep on this track along the edge of the wood, ignoring a bridleway entering from the left. There is a fine old woodland hedge on the left, made up of hazel, blackthorn, field maple, oak, wild rose, dogwood, sycamore, yew and box bushes – well worth a dating exercise (see Day 3).

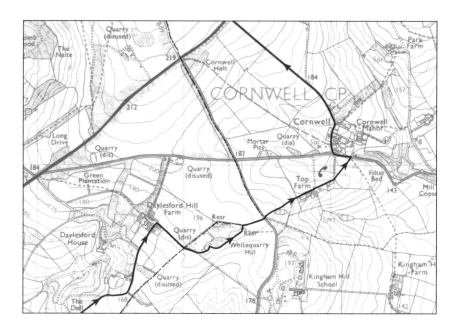

Enter Daylesford Hill Farm courtyard, and pass Hill Farm Cottage on the right to turn right along the footpath, with a beautiful view of the Evenlode valley to the right. The county boundary comes up the hill across open country, and crosses the track. Enter **Oxfordshire** and walk ahead, but at the fork in the track bear right to descend the slope. Fifty yards on, turn left along the woodland edge on a grassy bank.

There were wild flowers in profusion in August: marjoram, scabious, mullein, knapweed, harebells and pretty, pink-and-white striped columbine. Small tortoise-shell butterflies were feeding on the knapweed and scabious. In November, a 'charm' (flock) of goldfinches were feeding on the thistle seeds.

The county boundary joins us from the left near the end of the wood. At the fork of the footpaths, take the left-hand path to the road keeping in the same direction of travel (E 078°). There, turn left and after a few paces, right, through double, wooden gates onto a footpath down the hill. The hillside town of **Chipping Norton** can be seen to the right. Go through the farmyard of Top Farm, keeping to the left of the buildings and past the house. Where the drive turns left, cross a stile into the park-land of **Cornwell Manor**. Bear left downhill (NE 049°), aiming left of the gate piers.

Cornwell

The village architecture of **Cornwell** was restored by Clough Williams-Ellis, well known for designing the Italianate village of Portmeirion in Wales. Portmeirion tableware has since become famous.

Descend with care the steps to the road and turn left, though it is worth taking a few paces to the right first to look through the main gateway to admire the architecture of Cornwell Manor.

At the telephone box and road junction, turn right (N) along the road signposted 'Moreton-in-Marsh', past a farmyard full of ducks and hens and a sign to the church.

Access Point: Cornwell, 5 miles. Telephone, limited parking by small triangular green north of village. GR 270273.

Bear left at the small green to walk up the road flanked by ancient ash trees, and cross the B436 Stow-on-the-Wold road. Continue (NW 310°) on the left side of the hedge of the bridleway; 450 yards on from the road a bank is reached. Bear slightly left and enter the grassy enclosure which is Chastleton Barrow.

On leaving the enclosure by the northern entrance (left of the stables), it is possible to see that the ramparts were built of stones as some of them have rolled down into the path. Walk alongside the fence to cross the drive. The county boundary, with Gloucestershire to the west and Oxfordshire to the east, follows the road. We walked parallel to the boundary by going through the gate and walking downhill about

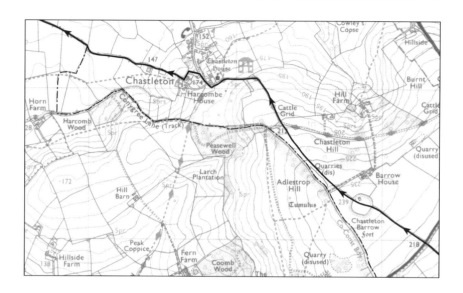

Chastleton Barrow

Chastleton Barrow

Despite its name, Chastleton Barrow is not a burial place but an oval-shaped enclosure of about three to four acres, with ramparts (banks) on which grow ancient trees. It is similar to the hill forts in Northamptonshire which had one or two farmsteads within them. Probably this was the house of a chieftain of the surrounding area in the Pre-Roman Iron Age (800 BC to 43 AD). On looking at the parish boundary of Chastleton you will see that it sticks out like a tongue into Warwickshire at this point. It has been suggested that this formed the original Iron Age estate based on Chastleton and Chastleton Barrow. It is an indication that some of the boundaries in this part of Oxfordshire date back to the Pre-Roman Iron Age.

100 yards away from the left field wall. At the bottom of the field, bear right to leave it by a small wooden gate. For those wishing to walk on the boundary, turn left at the drive, then right down the road. The boundary demonstrates the typical characteristics of an ancient way, for it is curving and has old beech trees bordering it, with other species of ancient woodland such as the wych elm.

Turn sharp right following the road, then left to continue north west down the hill towards **Chastleton**. On descending the hill, the dovecote in front of Chastleton House can be seen to the left side of the road. There was formerly a house there, but now only the dovecote remains.

Follow the road round to the left past the post-box to turn left into a no-through road.

Access Point: Chastleton, 6.8 miles. Limited parking near telephone at road junction 300 yards further north. GR 247294.

The watershed of the Cotswold Hills is being approached. It runs from Bourton-on-the-Hill, north of Moreton-in-Marsh, west of our position, to the Rollright Stones to the east. The scarp slope with its limestone beds dipping back towards Chastleton has a clay layer under the limestone which, by forming an impermeable barrier, forces the water to the surface to produce springs such as at Hill Farm (GR 259288) and in Chastleton village. These springs are tributaries of the River Evenlode and the Thames Basin. The River Stour (see Day 2) flows northwards to the River Avon and out to the Bristol Channel. There are fine views from here to Brailes Hill on the northern borders of the Cotswolds.

Chastleton House

Chastleton House was bought in 1604 by Walter Jones, a rich merchant, from Robert Catesby, who used the money to finance the Gunpowder Plot with Guy Fawkes. The plan is very unusual. It is extremely compact and consists of four storeys and a basement. The first floor has the Great Hall and the Parlour, and above it is the Long Gallery for exercise. There are two turrets, both of which contain staircases, and there is a service wing on the west side which has the brewhouse and stables. The house is built of the local orange ironstone or marlstone. The dressings are in a grey Chipping Norton limestone. The gardens have fine topiary hedges and it was here that the rules of croquet were codified. The house was inhabited by the Jones family for 400 years and is a remarkable example of an unchanged Jacobean house complete with its furnishings. The reason is that the Jones family was never rich enough to afford to rebuild in the latest architectural fashion. They also suffered badly in the 17th century as they were on the 'wrong' (Royalist) side and were fined during the Civil War. Although they recovered their estates, (Middle Brookend Farm, that we pass later in the day, was part of the Chastleton estate), they never really prospered and never made rich marriages, so the family gently declined in the 18th and 19th centuries until by the middle of the 19th century, three people were being looked after by two servants, compared to the Duke of Marlborough at Blenheim, who was employing 150 servants. Owned by the National Trust – Tel: 01494 755572 (bookings), 01494 755560 (information line).

The former fishponds that supplied Chastleton House can be seen to the right of the no-through road. At the farm, turn right downhill on a track. At a double bend, almost 800 yards on from the farm, by two large ash trees, the county boundary joins the track from the left. We are now walking on the boundary of Gloucestershire (left) and Oxfordshire (right).

This is an ancient curved track, with multi-specied hedges — we saw bright-pink spindle berries in December with the reds of the hawthorn berries and bryony fruits. There are field maples, oak, and ancient layered and pollarded ash trees. We saw a group of yellowhammers feeding in these hedges.

Continue for nearly 0.5 miles to where a bridleway crosses the track, go through the steel gate (NW 288°) and along the left side of the ancient hedgerow, still the county boundary. Go on for another 0.5 miles before leaving the bridleway.

In fine weather there are good views of the Cotswold Hills from this position. To the west, the villages of **Evenlode** and **Longborough** can be seen with the town of **Stow-on-the-Wold** to the south west. To the north west, **Bourton-on-the-Hill**, with its square church tower, and the great houses of **Sezincote** and **Batsford Park**, with its church spire, are visible. Closer to hand, in the field to our left, the rounded pebbles are the water-worn remains of glacial moraine left behind by the retreating ice. When the track between the hedge and fence ends (GR 231300), there is a field gate ahead with a stile on the right, one field short of Stuphill Covert. Turn right over the stile and follow the left side of the hedge to cross a footbridge over a small brook in the field corner. Cross the next field to a stile in the opposite hedge. Continue (NE 065°) on the right side of the hedge to cross the farm track leading to the wooden building, still called Tithe Barn. Go over the stile on the far side of the track to follow the path (NE) on the right side of the hedge. Cross a double stile in the corner of the next field.

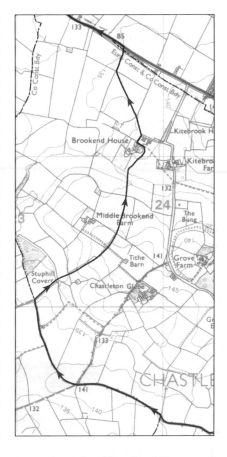

Walk across the next field (N 018°), aiming to the right of Brookend House and keeping parallel to the right hedge. Go through three steel gates. This is an area of springs, and limestone rock outcrops can be seen just before the second gate. In this next field, bear slightly right (040°) to aim for the right side of a small copse. Follow the wood around the pond to the left, and go through a steel gate to turn left onto a farm track. Keep right of a stone barn, pass a cottage, and turn right onto the farm drive. Walk under three large pine trees on the right side then, where the drive bends right, leave it by going through the steel gate. Bear left (NW 342°) across the field to cross a double stile and footbridge, and in the next field go diagonally left in the same direction to a railing fence in the far field corner.

From the stile, bear right (030°) across the field to reach a gate and implement sheds, and then the A44 road. By turning left onto the northern roadside path, we walk back into **Warwickshire**, the second shire that we entered at the beginning of

The county boundary is the thick line of trees to the right. We are now in the narrow northwesterly 'tongue' of Oxfordshire.

the Seven Shires Way. However, within 400 yards the county boundary crosses the road and follows a narrow belt of woodland. It is on the far side of a large ditch and bank. We could find no sign of the boundary stone (BS) marked on the map near here. Pass Heath Farm, with its beautiful stone farm buildings and dovecote, where the county boundary goes through their living room! Walk past an 18th century milestone on the south side of the road which says, 'Norton 10, Moreton 2'. Walk past North Four Shire Stone Farm (where the farmer's wife told us the tale of the Roman soldier who haunts this part of the road), then past the turning to Evenlode to the left, to arrive back at the Four Shire Stone. This is the formal end to the walk. To reach the car parking venue and railway station, walk towards **Moreton-in-Marsh** past the Fire Service Technical College, and subsequently to the estate roads on the right of the main road on the edge of Moreton-in-Marsh.

On reaching the speed restriction sign and the sign for the London road, turn right into a housing estate for parking.

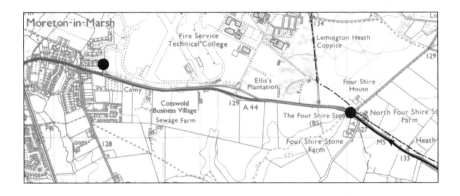

If black smoke is billowing out from the College, there is no need for alarm: it is holding a practice drill! Aeroplanes, vehicles and buildings are all set alight for training.

**We have walked the circuit three times, each in different seasons.
We hope you enjoy the days as much as we did.**